1 *(overleaf)* Somersetshire Buildings in Milsom Street, 1788

BATH

John Haddon

AQVAE · SVLIS

B. T. Batsford Ltd
London

© *John Haddon* 1973
First published 1973

ISBN 0 7134 0078 1

Printed and bound at
The Pitman Press, Bath
for the publishers
B. T. *Batsford Ltd,* 4 *Fitzhardinge Street*
*London W*1H 0*AH*

To The Goddess Sul-Minerva

and to

Alderman Bill Gallop, without whom this project would not have started but who is not to be blamed for the result; John Kite and his unfailingly helpful staff at the Bath Reference Library; Bob Bryant who is doing such splendid work on the City Archives; Tony Wyth, for his help on the history of planning; Neville Pearce, for expert and instant information about administrative structure; Peter Coard, who taught me much about the details of architecture; Michael Owen, for authoritative and friendly help on Roman Bath; The members of my WEA classes for whom much of this material was gathered, and whose friendly questions made me gather more; Margaret and Sally who patiently endured the mental and physical absenteeism that authorship involves;
And all the others who have helped—
John Haddon, author, fulfils his vows.

Acknowledgements

The author and publishers wish to thank the following for permission to reproduce the photographs included in this book: Aerofilms Ltd for figs 10, 25, 26, 44; Author's Collection for figs 3, 34, 40; Bath Public Library for figs 4, 5, 7, 9, 11, 15, 19, 20, 21, 22, 27, 28, 32, 35, 37, 38, 39; Bath & Wiltshire Chronicle and Herald for figs 41, 42; B. T. Batsford Photographic Collection for figs 1, 12, 13, 23, 31; British Museum for fig 14; Hunting Surveys Ltd for fig 2; A. F. Kersting for figs 6, 17, 18; Radio Times Hulton Picture Library for figs 8, 24, 29, 30, 33, 36; Henk Snoek & Associates for fig 43; the Trustees of the Victoria and Albert Museum for fig 16; and to Noel Habgood for the photograph reproduced on the cover. Thanks are also due to The Society of Antiquaries and Professor B. W. Cunliffe, for the drawings on pages 22 and 25 which are taken from the Society's Research Report No. 24, *Roman Bath;* and to Geographia Ltd. and Her Majesty's Stationery Office for permission to reproduce the map on pages viii–ix.

Contents

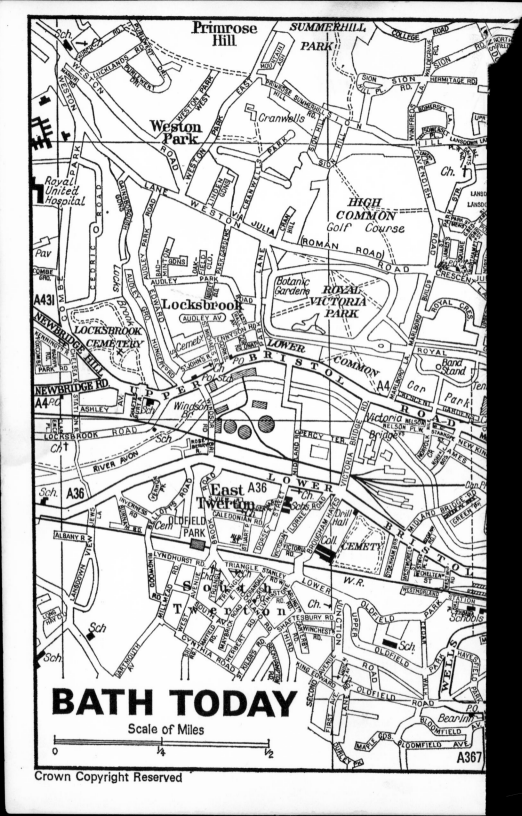

BATH TODAY

Scale of Miles

0   1/4   1/2

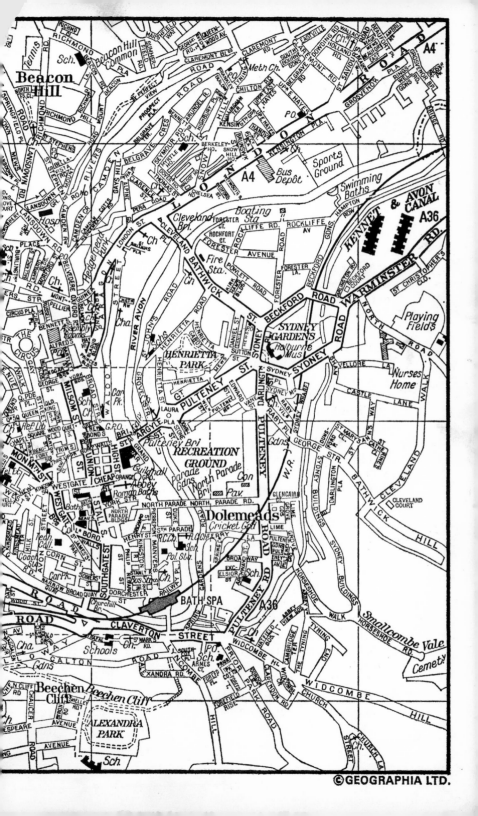

© GEOGRAPHIA LTD.

The Illustrations

Maps and Diagrams

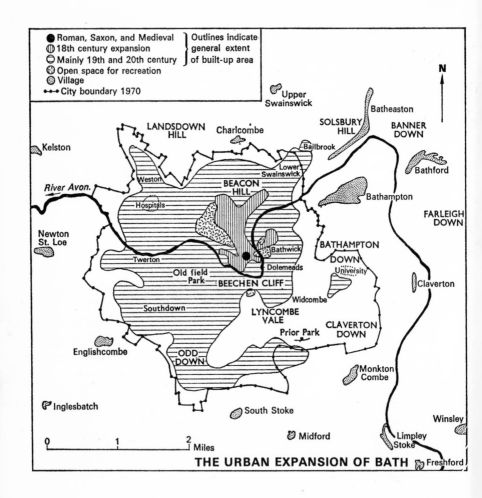

N

Upper
Swainswick

Batheaston

SOLSBURY
HILL

BANNER
DOWN

LANDSDOWN
HILL

Charlcombe

Bailbrook

Kelston

Bathford

Lower
Swainswick

River Avon.

Weston

BEACON
HILL

Bathampton

FARLEIGH
DOWN

Hospitals

Newton
St. Loe

Bathwick

BATHAMPTON
DOWN

Twerton

Dolemeads

University

Claverton

Old field
Park

BEECHEN CLIFF

Widcombe

Southdown

LYNCOMBE
VALE

CLAVERTON
DOWN

Prior Park

Englishcombe

ODD
DOWN

Monkton
Combe

Inglesbatch

South Stoke

Winsley

0   1   2
⌞_____⌟_____⌟ Miles

Midford

Limpley
Stoke

THE URBAN EXPANSION OF BATH

Freshford

1 *The Beginnings*
Prehistoric Bath

The City of Bath, said Walter Chapman, its Mayor in 1663, was on a batch in a bottom. A batch derives from the same Old English root as 'back'. In Somerset it signifies a low ridge or hill – tips from the coal mines are 'dirt batches' – and the batch in Bath, although it appears in no name, is a little platform, a fragment of river terrace left from the time when the valley bottom stood some five metres higher than today. Just high enough to keep out of the floods, just wide enough to give a modest building area before steep hillsides began to rear, it would have been suitable for a village, or a small town, except for one thing – from thousands of feet below the surface, where the splitting atoms concentrate their heat, there welled up without ceasing a morass-making welter of hot water.

This hill-girt region of dense forest, swamp, and frightening vapour, was no place for prehistoric man. Indeed, it may be questioned whether it has ever been a good site for a city, which makes Bath even more of a miracle. Archaeological evidence indicates that on the eve of a Roman invasion Iron Age men of a tribe the Romans called the Dobunni were occupying hill forts above the valley. The best to see today is on Little Solsbury hill, but the largest was on Bathampton Down. Environmentally these were the best sites, with clean air, accessible springs, a lightly-wooded country not too difficult to clear for their small plots or to use as pasture for their herds and flocks, and admirably situated for defence. But these folk were not savages. They had a culture which though different was not necessarily inferior to Rome's, they were intelligent and imaginative people, and there is nothing improbable in their having discovered something of the healing properties of the waters, or of developing in some rudimentary form their use, or of enshrining the mysterious misty locality in some religious cult. For they had a goddess, Sul, and when the Romans placed Bath under the protection of Minerva they were sufficiently sensitive to local feeling to amalgamate her, as we shall see, with that ancient presiding deity in the form of Sul-Minerva. And then there is the legend.

For as long as people could remember, the citizens of Bath had been certain about the origin of their City and it was not until the seventeenth-century Age of Reason that they became doubtful of their apparently unsophisticated story. This incensed the great architect of early eighteenth-century Bath, John Wood, who determined to give it the authority of print and set it out in all its detail – with a few ideas of his own – in his *Essay Towards a Description of Bath* (1765). Unfortunately he was a historian credulous, opinionated, and fanciful, reading widely but uncritically, rejecting what did not fit his own thesis. The story, according to Wood, and without comment, is as follows.

In the year 744 BC Brutus (or Brut) with a company of fellow Trojans landed near Totnes and having defeated the local giants carved himself out a kingdom from the Tamar to the boundaries of Wiltshire and Gloucestershire. Seventh in line from Brutus came King Hudibras whose only son, Bladud, 'a most ingenious young Prince', unfortunately contracted leprosy. The Court, who naturally did not want to get leprosy too, petitioned the King to banish the young man, which he did. The Queen gave her son a ring so that if he ever came back, unrecognisable, he could identify himself.

2 Little Solsbury Hill with Iron Age Camp

3 Bladud as Abaris the Sage; plaque in Cross Bath

4 The Gorgon's Head

And so the young prince wandered away and took the only occupation which seems available to princes in legends – he became a swineherd. This was at Keynsham a few miles from Bath. Unfortunately the pigs caught his leprosy and to delay its discovery he got permission to take the herd up the Avon valley to feed on the acorns in the woods. Crossing the river at Swineford he passed the hot springs with some difficulty because the pigs were so delighted with the 'warm ouzy bed' that he could only get them away by tempting them with acorns 'slightly strewed before them'. Moving on they settled at Swineswick (modern Swainswick) where he built a separate shelter for each pig to try to stop the infection spreading. When he washed the pigs he noted some had shed their 'hoary marks' but he did not then connect this with the wallowing. A few days later, however, he lost one of his best sows. She had been missing for a week when he accidentally came across her back at the wallow – and when he washed her he saw that her leprosy had gone. This time, for he was no fool, he saw the connection, and, stripping off, flung himself into the mud. Every day after when he had driven the pigs into the wood to feed he went back to the springs, and in a few days he was cured.

Hurrying back to Keynsham he told the whole story to his master who, not unnaturally, thought he was mad but after a while was prevailed on to accompany the Prince to the Court where Bladud created a sensation by slipping the jewel (which we have not forgotten) into the Queen's drink. Recognised and acclaimed, Bladud decided that it would be too embarrassing to stay at that time amongst the people who had caused his banishment so he applied to his father for study-leave abroad and, refusing any retinue or pomp, set out for Athens. This was in 505 BC and he spent eleven years abroad, where he was known as Abaris, the Northern Sage, instructing the Persian Zoroaster in magic and the Greek Pythagoras in philosophy, notably teaching him the sun-centred nature of the planetary system. Both Zoroaster and Pythagoras then retired into caves to ponder their new learning. Abaris also reconstructed the temple at Delphi and did other building works. His form of transport was a magic flying Arrow which he eventually presented to Pythagoras, but Wood suggests that this was really a symbol of his teaching. The Arrow became the Northern Constellation and as the next one is the Eagle 'is it not highly probable', said Wood, 'that the Eagle is Abaris who, as Bladud, made wings to fly with and decked himself with feathers? Indeed, did not his name come from *Blas*, a knowledge of the motions of the stars, and *dud* because he was held to be a "meer Dudman" in his fancy feathers?'

Back in Britain, or Albion, Bladud succeeded his father and for his capital built in 483 BC the city of Caerbrent, otherwise known as Caer Ennaint, the City of Ointment, Caer Yrn Naint Twymin, the City of the Warm Vale, Caer Palladur, the City of Pallas's Water, Troy Novant, the Turning Valley, Caer Badon, the City of the Bath, Aquae Solis, Waters of the Sun, Aquae Calidae, Hot Waters, Bathancester, the Baths, Hatbathan, the Hot Baths, and Ackmanchester, the place of the Oak Men in reference to the Druids, Bath being the Metropolitan Seat of these priests. Indeed, Bladud founded a University for Druids at nearby Stanton Drew whose standing stones Wood proved to his own satisfaction were a model of the solar system. It was, says Wood, their heretical belief in the sun-centred system which led to the suppression of the Druids by the Roman church. This and a great deal more about the 'Oakmen' is very great nonsense but the eighteenth century was fascinated by Druids and saw them all over the place.

Bladud came to a spectacular end. Inspired perhaps by his experiences on his Arrow he made himself wings, cast himself off the Temple of Apollo 'and was thereby dashed to pieces'. He was succeeded by his son, King Lear, in 463 BC. Later the line died out, there was civil war, and a new dynasty added even more magnificence to Bath, until the Romans came, knocked it about and slaughtered the Druids.

Under Agricola, says Wood, the town was rebuilt, the Druids came back for a time, and the new British King there was King Coil (Coel, or Cole).

Everything after the story of the pigs is either plain impossible or so wildly improbable as to be discounted. And yet it would be rash to dismiss a legend without definite proof of falsehood for it may contain some clue, however slight, to ancient and oral tradition concealed in the accretions, inventions, and imitative mythology of later centuries. It is certainly not impossible that the efficacy of a local mud-pack was discovered in pre-Roman days by observation of its effect on domestic animals and this could well lead to a local cult of healing. The disease could not have been leprosy but we must remember that the term was used to cover a whole variety of milder skin diseases.

There is one other proposition which is just possible although unproven and not generally accepted. This is Wood's contention that Lansdown hill reaching down to the north side of the city is that Mount Badon where Arthur traditionally fought his last great victorious battle against the Saxon invaders. One thing in favour of this and of the pig story is that they are the two things which Wood does not attempt to prove.

At least three statues commemorated Bladud in Bath. Those at the King's and Cross Baths can still be seen, but the third disappeared when the North Gate was pulled down in the eighteenth century. This last statue was apparently a very poor affair and contrasted sadly with two new effigies on the Guildhall of 1625 celebrating King Edgar and, according to Wood, King Cole, which, now sadly worn, may be seen on a house at the end of Bath Street. The contrast caused some indignation at the beginning of the eighteenth century and inspired the Deputy Town Clerk to verse, in which King Bladud's Ghost exclaims:

'Two upstart Princes of a modern Race,
Our ent'ring Street with dazling Splendour Grace',

while he himself is crowned with cobwebs and has no clothes.

'In Vain (he cries) you may my further Aid invoke,
I am so mean that all Men think I'm broke.'

So let the Council –

'Discharge the Debt of Honour so long due,
That I may shine as well as t'other two.'

Polemic poetry is out of fashion, although there is no lack of Protest songs. It could be revived for the present controversy in Bath over the Buchanan traffic plan with its approach roads and tunnel. Many pamphlets and letters for and against have been produced but no one has so far invoked the shade of John Wood in verse. It could be done – for instance (it does not have to be good poetry):

Did I a grand Palladian Town design for you,
Only to have a Monst'rous Highway driven through?

Or, contrariwise,

Curs't Horseless Carriage clutt'ring up the Road?
Be banish'd to the Netherworld, your just Abode.

After Bladud we enter authentic history, however patchy the evidence and however susceptible to variety of interpretation. It is a story which begins with a Roman road.

2 *Aquae Sulis*
Roman Bath

The Emperor Claudius, who, stammering and twitching, had by feigning foolishness remained alive, and by appearing harmless been raised by the Praetorian Guard to the Imperial purple, was in need of a military Triumph. And what more inspiring achievement than to extend the bounds of Rome to that mysterious, misty island which lay beyond steel-grey Ocean where no land should be! A triumph indeed to succeed where nearly a hundred years before the great Julius had attempted no more than a rather unimpressive show of force and where mad Caligula only a few years ago had got no further than collecting seashells at Boulogne!

As a bid for prestige the scheme was not without shrewdness, but there were other reasons as well. The Channel was not a good frontier. It was an escape route for dissident Gauls, and from beyond it the Britons were making rude gestures with impunity. Moreover, not only were the British getting too powerful to be comfortable neighbours, but they were also revealing themselves in trade as occupants of a land of some importance for grain and metals – and the Empire fed its economy not on raising productivity, but on extending its realm.

And so in AD 43 there assembled, presumably somewhere on the Calais coast, an invasion force of some forty or fifty thousand men under the able command of Aulus Plautius, summoned from the Governorship of Pannonia (Hungary). The backbone of the army was formed of four infantry legions – the II Augusta from Argentoratum (Strasbourg), the XX Valeria from Novaesium (Neuss), the XIV Gemina from Moguntiacum (Mainz), and the IX Hispania who had come with Plautius from Pannonia. The rest of the fighting force, including the cavalry, consisted of the lower-paid auxiliaries recruited from the provinces. It was a tough, experienced band of professionals to whom fighting was a business and the Army a home. When it heard where it was going it expressed its disapproval in no uncertain terms and for a moment mutiny was in the air. Then someone made a joke and the army got on with the job of preparing to take the eagles 'outside the limit of the known world'.

Crossing at night and landing, in all likelihood, at Dover, Lympne and Richborough (we do not know for certain), the legions probably concentrated at Canterbury. They then forced the Medway crossing, fought their way to the Thames and reached the northern swamps by bridge. How much further they advanced we cannot be sure before Aulus Plautius sent for Claudius, who arrived with elephants some six weeks later, and entered Camulodunum, capital of the Catuvellauni, where according to the inscription on his arch in Rome he received the surrender of eleven kings. After 16 days in Britain, Claudius returned to Rome for his Triumph and left Aulus Plautius to get on with the task of securing the new piece of Empire.

It must be emphasised that for the invasion the literary sources are slender and the archaeological ones patchy. This leaves the way open for a variety of interpretations. One point which is perhaps relevant to the west is the report that 'When these kings had fled he (Aulus Plautius) won over by agreement a portion of the Bodunni, a people dependent on the Catuvellauni; thereupon he left a garrison there and continued his advance. Then he came to a river.' The river was most likely the Medway; what is curious is that the Bodunni are nowhere else ever mentioned and it seems probable that this is a mistake for the Dobunni, especially as the northern part of the tribe under Boduocus seems to have favoured Rome. But if it was the Dobunni, what were they doing around the Medway? Had Boduocus, backing the Romans to win, made sure that his envoys were early on the spot? Or is it possible that against all probability and the best opinion, the landing was in the west? Or, as seems most likely, was this simply the surrender of a band levied by Caractacus from the Gloucestershire tribe?

From Camulodunum the legions fanned out, probing into tribal territory. To the west came the 2nd Augusta under the future Emperor Vespasian and it is possible that this advance was started even before Claudius had arrived, for its progress was swift and Vespasian was back in Rome for the triumph of AD 44. Swift, but not unopposed, for while most tribes quickly capitulated the Durotriges and the southern Dobunni resisted from their hill forts. The notable example is of course the great stronghold of Maiden Castle, but there is also evidence from the Somerset forts of Cadbury, Ham Hill, and Worlebury. Nevertheless the west was subjugated and by AD 47, when his term of office was finished and he handed over his Province to Ostorius Scapula, Aulus Plautius had established a frontier zone, or *limes*, which stretched from Exeter to Gloucester, across the Midlands to Leicester and Lincoln and the Humber. Along this zone was being driven the great road later to be known as the Fosse Way and it is to this road that we owe the first town of Bath.

The Fosse has its mysteries. We do not know for certain when it was started – it could have been several years after AD 47 – and we cannot be sure that it was designed as one road and built as one operation. For example, at Cirencester it does not cross the Silchester–Gloucester Ermine Street directly but runs along it for a quarter of a mile before heading off for Leicester and Lincoln. There is also the question of Akeman Street. This was the name given to the road from the NE Fosse to St Albans and London and also to the Fosse between Bath and Cirencester; moreover one of the Saxon names for Bath was Akemanceaster (others were Bathanceaster and Hat Batha). It would be nice to think that the name arose from the aches carried down the road for cure at Bath but this is etymologically unsound and it is more likely to be based on a personal name or derived from 'Aquae (Sulis)'. We can therefore either think of the Fosse as one great frontier road from near Axminster in Devon to the Humber, or as three roads, Lincoln–Cirencester, Axminster–Bath, Bath–Cirencester (possibly in that order of building), or as two, Axminster–Cirencester and Cirencester–Lincoln. Whichever we choose we still have the problems that although we know the entry and exit we cannot trace the road through Bath itself, and that there are *two* southern approaches, for in addition to the route which became the main Fosse, coming into Bath down Holloway and crossing the river near the present bridge, there was another branch (or earlier line?) which curved away along the southern hills to the old Iron Age camp on Bathampton Down.

Whatever the problems, it seems certain that throughout the middle of the first century there was a major Roman road descending the hills south of Bath by means of the later Holloway, crossing the river, climbing gently through the steaming swamp to the river terrace and then following the river valley out along the line of the present London road. Moreover at least three other roads converged on the area. Two were probably of no great importance and have left but small traces. The first was an alternative route to Cirencester, following the old Jurassic Way up Lansdown; the second came up, probably from Poole, via Frome, to join the Fosse at Odd Down on the southern plateau; and the third came in from the port of Abonae (Sea Mills) on the Avon, joined the Fosse in the present parish of Walcot and left it again at Batheaston, where it crossed the river and headed for Marlborough to join the road to Silchester and London. Sea Mills would have been a major supply point for Roman activities in South Wales and it is likely that it had a busy London Road. Was there a military camp at the intersection of the two roads near Bath? The probability is that there was and that it lies in the present parish of Walcot, but there is no direct evidence.

It was not, however, the arts of war which brought the town into being but those of peace. Give a Roman a quarter of a million gallons of hot mineral water a day and he knew what to do with it – bathe! And he had the engineering, plumbing, and building techniques to achieve his object. Caractacus had said of the Romans during his last stand in the Welsh mountains, 'They make a desolation and call it peace', but of Bath it might be said that 'They found a morasse and made of it a place of pleasure'.

Some 30–40 years after the invading armies had landed the great springs were encapsulated and controlled, and on the hardening land there arose before the eyes of the doubtless amazed Dobunni stone upon gleaming stone of new-cut ashlar as the palaces of health, cleanliness, games and godliness thrust their Mediterranean shapes into an alien air. From the hills around came the great blocks of oolite, the Bath stone, soft in the quarry, hard in the air, white at birth and ageing to a golden grey, cutting smoothly under the chisel. From the mines of Mendip, 30 miles to the south-west, came the pigs of lead to be melted in the furnace rediscovered only in 1970 and cast in sheets to make the pipes and line the reservoir and the Great Bath, which would alone have required about 90 pigs. The wooded Avon valley provided the timbers for constructional work, particularly the roofing of the first bathing establishment, and also locally available was clay for tiles and limestone for the remarkable Roman concrete. It made an impact and a disturbance even greater than a present-day motorway construction on an ancient and isolated village. What they built was to stand in pride and prosperity for 400 years.

And then it vanished. Slowly and without drama, but surely and inexorably the roofs collapsed, the walls fell in, the columns toppled, and the waters embalmed the remains in mud. Roman fragments were hauled out and used to fill a gap or patch a wall, but the rest was lost to sight and a whole new town spread its streets and buildings many feet above the foundations of Aquae Sulis – the Roman city is some 10–15 feet below present ground level. In medieval times the same springs were used but the baths were new; and when in the eighteenth century John Wood set out to recreate Roman glory in Bath he had no conception of the realities of the Roman city. Our knowledge of Roman Bath has depended mainly on the right man having been on the spot when a deep hole was dug.

For the interested visitor it is unfortunate that these holes were usually made in preparation for buildings which then sealed off the site but there is also the lucky chance that when in 1871 the King's Bath, which lay directly over the Roman reservoir, sprang a leak the person responsible for trenching down, the City Engineer Major Charles Edward Davis, was a man of antiquarian interests and was assisted by a builder, Richard Mann, who was also deeply interested and kept very detailed records and plans of part of the discoveries. Davis's pumps, however, were working so efficiently that they were also draining the nearby Kingston Baths and further work was stopped until 1878 when the Corporation acquired the property. The new excavations aroused considerable local interest and funds were raised to buy adjacent property.

It is to the local interest of our Victorian forbears and to the energies of Major Davis that we owe the preservation for public view of a Roman remain of international importance. Whether Charles Edward Davis was the best man for the job, however, is a matter of conjecture; certainly at the time he aroused acrimonious opposition which culminated in an attempt to have him removed as local secretary of the Society of Antiquaries by a resolution to its Council in 1886. The opposition seems to have centred around Mr Mann who had quarrelled with Davis and accused him in print of obstructing his own archaeological work, misinterpreting the finds, and vandalising the baths by destruction and concealment. The most vitriolic attack came at the time of the British Association's meeting at Bath in 1888 when a Mr Frederick Vinson wrote a letter to the paper which included the words '. . . they [the BA] are confronted with the notice "No Roman antiquities have been hidden or destroyed, Charles E Davis FSA". For cool effrontery perhaps this can hardly be surpassed. Nor is the position of affairs improved by Sir John Lubbock's discovery of Mr Davis's "modesty", a characteristic hitherto wholly unsuspected.' Davis himself appears to have maintained a dignified silence, at any rate in print.

The main trouble was that he had been commissioned to build a modern suite of treatment rooms, of which he was very proud and whose construction involved him in disturbing and covering up a less impressive but archaeologically very important part of the Roman establishment. His treatment centre, an interesting but now useless piece of Victoriana, has been demolished to be replaced by a neo-Georgian block – giving opportunity for further, if limited discovery. The other major difficulty is that Davis did not keep sufficiently detailed records of the excavation. On balance, however, it seems only fair to say that, in spite of undoubted deficiencies, Davis's work is such that we have cause to be grateful to him. Prebendary Scarth speaking at University College [*sic*] Bristol said, 'I . . . can only say how much has been due to the energy and perseverance of the city architect, Major Davis', and more recently Professor Barry Cunliffe in his definitive work on Roman Bath has written: 'Looking at the remains today, however, it is surprising how little damage was done . . . the structures found, together with their latest floor-levels, are by and large intact and ready to yield new information.' So we can certainly give the Major two cheers, if not three.

When the visitor descends to the Roman level he passes the Circular Bath and sees before him the Great Bath.

Round this runs a Victorian colonnade with a Victorian balustrade supporting mouldering Victorian statues of Roman emperors – an alternative to the other idea put forward at the time that the whole thing should be roofed in glass and iron like a railway station. Looking eastward along the length of the bath he sees that the establishment continues under the paving to the south of the Abbey and there he will find a further bath (the 'Lucas') and a complex of other structures. This far end is not a Davis hole and deserves some comment. At one time there stood above it the Abbey Church House. This was demolished in 1755 to make way for the Duke of Kingston's baths and excavation showed first a Saxon cemetery and then below it Roman foundations which were carefully recorded by Dr Charles Lucas (hence the name of the bath) assisted by the architect John Wood (of whom a good deal more later). There was no move to preserve these and they were quickly covered by the new bathing establishment. This, in its turn, was demolished in 1923 and the Roman remains excavated and described by W. H. Knowles. And so the matter rested until 1954 when the Spa Committee asked Sir Ian Richmond to supervise the preparation of the area for display. He did more, and by the time of his death in 1965 had worked out plans, descriptions and sequences for the whole length apart from the western complex by and beyond the Circular Bath.

No other hole is now open to visitors but in the Baths Museum may be seen fascinating Roman fragments from the subterranean city. A number of these relate to the nearby temple of Sul-Minerva, a building of such importance that it is of interest to note briefly some of the excavation history. To the north of the Roman Baths lies the Pump Room. It is now part of the whole building complex and from it you can look straight across the King's Bath to the hall of the Great Bath. The Pump Room was rebuilt as part of the Improvements of 1790 and in digging deep for foundations a pavement, wall, flight of steps and a number of sculptured stones were uncovered. These remains included a remarkable Gorgon's Head whose workmanship, vitality, and unusual beard and moustaches suggest British work on a Classical subject. These remains were recognised as those of a temple but were, of course, built over.

Opposite the Pump Room on the western side of Stall Street lay the White Hart Hotel which in 1867 was pulled down to be replaced by the flamboyant Grand Pump Room Hotel. The site was closely observed and minutely measured and recorded by James Irvine who was at that time employed by Sir Gilbert Scott to supervise restoration work on the Abbey. He recorded, among other things, a great slab of concrete which was the platform (*podium*) on which the temple had rested. Half of this is now buried in the modern concrete of Arlington House which replaced the hotel in 1959, and whose building gave little opportunity for further investigation apart from a quick rescue dig which confirmed the existence and alignment of the *podium* and disclosed a wall and hypocaust.

It would not be appropriate in a general work to describe all the other various small sites which have yielded clues to Roman Bath – they are summarised in the map, p. 16 – but some mention must be made of post-war activity. Bath is fortunate in receiving the attention of the Camerton Archaeological Society and its Director, Mr J. Wedlake and of being served by its own Excavation Committee (founded in 1963) working with Professor Barry Cunliffe and Mr Michael Owen, the Curator of the Baths. Archaeology is a passion and its work its own reward but it serves a wider purpose, not least to meet a deep psychological need to feel a contact with the past, a need which is not without economic results – witness the 500,000 visitors to the Baths within a year.

The work is not easy in Bath. Excavation of open sites is a race against time – for time is money to contractors – and subterranean digging, on which a good deal of our recent knowledge depends, is arduous in the extreme. Bath, particularly the centre, is a hollow city where buildings and

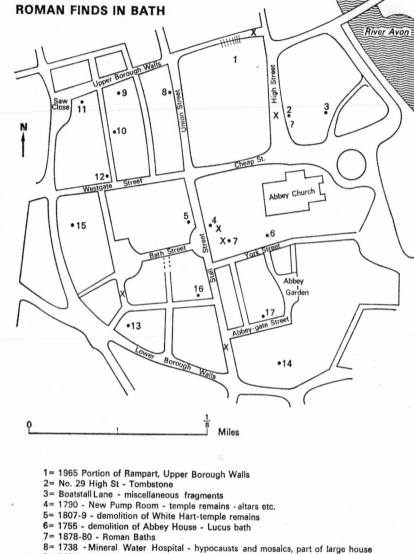

ROMAN FINDS IN BATH

River Avon

Upper Borough Walls

1

High Street

Saw Close

11

9

8

2
?

3

N

10

Cheap St.

12

Westgate Street

Abbey Church

5

4
X

15

X • 7

• 6

Bath Street

Stall Street

York Street

Abbey Garden

16

17

• 13

Abbey-gate Street

Lower Borough Walls

• 14

0   1 $\frac{1}{8}$ Miles

1= 1965 Portion of Rampart, Upper Borough Walls
2= No. 29 High St - Tombstone
3= Boatstall Lane - miscellaneous fragments
4= 1790 - New Pump Room - temple remains - altars etc.
5= 1807-9 - demolition of White Hart-temple remains
6= 1755 - demolition of Abbey House - Lucus bath
7= 1878-80 - Roman Baths
8= 1738 - Mineral Water Hospital - hypocausts and mosaics, part of large house
9= 1859 - Extension to Hospital - tesselated floor, etc.
10=1884 - Further extension - mosaic
11=1859 - rebuildings of Blue Coat school-mosaic
12=1814 - mosaic
13=1864 - Albert wing to Hospital-hypocausts mosaics. etc. of large establishments
14=1897 - Weymouth House Schools- mosaic
15=1964 - Third century building
16=1965 - Timber building succeded by stone one
17=1964 - Abbeygate Street - Roman house
X= Altars

streets rest upon a labyrinthine cellarage formed from the arches which raise the level ground floors above the mud and slopes. This means that a great deal of evidence, particularly medieval, has been removed or disturbed, and also that the archaeologist works for much of his time like 'a mole i' the cellarage', and a very hot, damp, cramped, mucky hole at that! It would indeed be splendid if we could realise Barry Cunliffe's dream of disembowelling Bath, supporting it on well-spaced pillars and revealing the Roman city as a netherworld; but such a venture would probably end up as an underground car-park.

The Abbey, however, has no cellars, which is a pity because it is sitting over the major part of a third important Roman building and we would like to know what this was. It stood facing the temple and was probably a theatre. Thus the city centred on a three-piece suite – temple, bathing house, and theatre(?) whose disposition is shown on the map, p. 18. If today you stand in the middle of the Abbey churchyard you can see to your north a range of eighteenth-century shops, to your east the (somewhat restored) six-teenth-century Abbey front, to your south the Pump Room in two blocks, late Victorian towards the Abbey, late Georgian towards the colonnade of 1790 which is to your west. Beyond the colonnade is Stall Street and postwar Arlington House. And if you were to sink through the paving for some fifteen feet you would be standing in the precinct of the (first-century?) Roman temple.

If now we imagine Roman Bath jacked-up to the present street level we can get some idea of the layout of the central area. Most of this is reconstruction and some is conjecture but in order to get a general picture we will not clutter the description with caveats – for detailed discussion and detective work the reader is referred to the publications of the Bath and Camerton Archaeological Society, the reports of the Bath Excavation Committee, and Barry Cunliffe's splendid book on *Roman Bath*. Let us assume that the temple was built about the same time or at any rate not much later

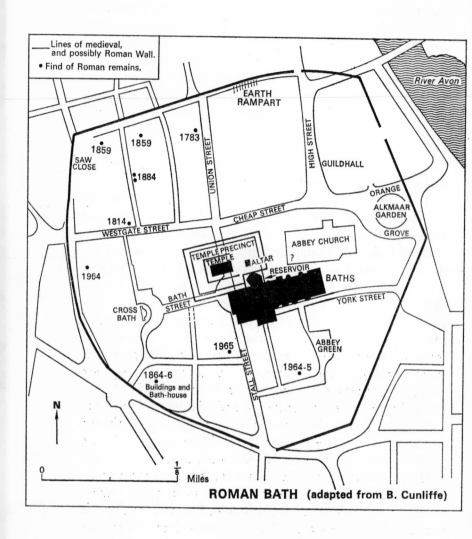

Lines of medieval, and possibly Roman Wall.

• Find of Roman remains.

River Avon

EARTH RAMPART

HIGH STREET

GUILDHALL

1859

1859

1783

UNION STREET

SAW CLOSE

•1884

ORANGE

ALKMAAR GARDEN

GROVE

1814

CHEAP STREET

WESTGATE STREET

ABBEY CHURCH

TEMPLE PRECINCT

TEMPLE

ALTAR

RESERVOIR

?

BATHS

1964

BATH STREET

YORK STREET

CROSS BATH

1965

ABBEY GREEN

STALL STREET

1964-5

1864-6

Buildings and Bath-house

N

0   ⅛   Miles

ROMAN BATH (adapted from B. Cunliffe)

than the baths and that we are viewing them when they were 'all new-and-all' about the end of the first century.

All round is the wall of a great rectangular paved precinct, about 250 feet long by about 160 wide. The north-east corner lies just east of the passage through to the High Street and the north wall runs westward through the shops, across Stall Street and to about 90 feet into the buildings on the other side. Here it turns south to its south-west corner in Bath Street and comes back along the street to the line of the north wall of the Baths. All along the inside of these walls is a colonnaded walk, some ten feet wide. The eastern side of the precinct is closed by a wall running south through the Pump Room entrance where just inside, and in line with the south-west door of the Abbey, is the grand two-arched entrance. The colonnade is here on the outside of this wall and at its south end is a platform and steps leading down to where the great culvert carrying unneeded water from the reservoir is open and the water can be drunk. This 'dipping-place' can still be seen by visitors to the Baths and the sight of the steamy water rushing from the wall is an impressive one. Not only is there a rectangular opening for the water but immediately above is an arched opening through which the steam ejects – a fine piece of organisation by the 'effects man'.

This eastern wall of the reservoir enclosure forms part of a massive rectangle which protrudes into the south-east part of the precinct, impressively breaking the line of the south wall and forming one of the four focal points of attention which are the entrance arches, the sacred spring, the altar, and the temple. On the north face of the wall is a monumental façade of six fluted pilasters supporting an entablature and an attic storey with a large triangular pediment decorated with the head of a moon goddess. In the wall panels between the pilasters, except for the centre, there are niches with sculptures representing the four seasons, although this is complete conjecture; we do not know *where* the Four Seasons stood nor if it incorporated the Luna pediment. In the centre, however, is a door reached by three large steps from the precinct floor. Open the door and step through, possibly on a platform, to see the sacred spring, its irregular octagonal wall nearly filling the enclosure. It is here that you may throw in some small token to keep the gods on your side – such as the small collection of gemstones discovered in the outlet, or the Bath Curse scratched on a lead plate, written backwards so that only a god would understand. Humans have tried various interpretations of which the most probable is: 'May he who carried off Vilbia from me become as liquid as water. [May] she who obscenely devoured her [become] dumb, whether Velvinna, Exsupereus, Verianus, Severinus, Augustalis, Comitianus, Germanilla [or] Jovina' – perhaps the gods made some sense of it!

Turning back and looking down the steps, flanked by short colonnades, we see in front of us a raised platform, about 15 by 20 feet, and on it the sacrificial altar with figures of gods and goddesses carved at each corner. If we stand close to the easternmost window of the old Pump Room we are standing above the site of the altar and if we then turn to look towards Stall Street, squinting along the front of the building, there, rising up in our mind's eye is the pillared portico of the temple, standing with the front of its six-foot high podium running down the west wall of the Pump Room for about 25 feet. Broad steps lead up to the tetrastyle (four-columned) portico of the sacred room, or *cella*, whose outside walls are decorated with attached columns. And above the portico, on the architrave supported by the 26-foot fluted Corinthian columns is the triangular pediment with the famous Gorgon's Head on a shield held by two buxom Victories balanced uneasily on globes, while in each of the bottom corners of the pediment 'old Triton blows his wreathed horn'. An idea of the appearance of the portico, though not of the temple, can be had from a pavilion in Sydney Gardens erected in 1909.

The temple and altar stand in an inner precinct which

round the temple is bordered by a low wall, possibly with columns standing on it, and round the altar is marked by a step down. In the precinct there are small altars in honour of the dead. These are dedicated to the presiding goddess Sul-Minerva. Sul was the pre-Roman goddess who the Romans with their customary broad-mindedness in these matters allowed to continue by identification with one of their own – in this case Minerva, a useful general-purpose deity who could handle most things loosely interpreted as art or science. An example, now in the Baths Museum, stood, although possibly not at this time, just to the west of the altar. It is a statue base and of particular interest because it is for an augurer (*haruspex*) who doubtless served in temple ceremonies – it reads 'Deae Sul L. Marcius Memor harusp[ex] d[ono] d[edit]'. For Minerva herself there is almost certainly at least one almost life-size gilded bronze statue, for its head was found in 1727 below Stall Street. That she has no top to her head probably indicates that her helmet was a separate casting.

Cleanliness is naturally next door to godliness but to reach it we have to go round the corner, passing between the Pump Room and the Abbey to the end wall of the Victorian parapet around the Baths. Standing at the end of this we are over the 'Lucas' Bath and the whole establishment runs back under the paving for about 90 feet, while at the far end it extends underground to the opposite side of the street. The south side of the establishment runs along the edge of York Street except at the west end where it projects beyond its far side. So much for position.

What we see with our first-century eyes is a long building with stone walls. Two-thirds of the way along, lying over Abbey Street, is the rectangular projection containing the main entrances and as far as this each side wall has four separate bulges or bays (*exedrae*) made by interior alcoves where bathers could sit. In front of us, at the east end, are two other entrance doors. Looking up we see the triangular end of a tiled timber roof which runs over the main entrance, where it meets a north–south roof which covers the entrance and entry hall. Beyond the entrance is a barrel-vault covering the west-end baths. The roof does not cover the whole width but rises up above the roofs of side aisles and between the main and aisle roofs the side walls are pierced with windows (see diagram).

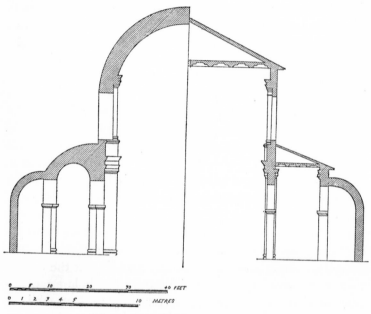

The roof construction of the Great Bath

Walking down the side and entering by the main door we pass through a short passage into a hall. In front of us are windows giving a view of the spring, on the right archways lead to the hall of the Great Swimming Bath and on our left is a suite of rooms which provide the more usual kind of Roman baths. These are rooms of different temperatures, the *caldarium* and *tepidarium*, with floors heated by hypocausts, flues formed by raising the floor on pillars (*pilae*) of stone or tile. Hot air for the hypocausts comes through from a furnace. There is also a small swimming bath (*natatio*) beside a dressing room (*apodyterium*). These western baths have a barrel-vault because of the danger of fire from the heating system. There is no such danger from the Great Bath and when we enter its hall we see a high timber roof supported on rectangular piers springing up from near the water's edge and a lower roof along the aisles. In the walls are the alcoves which we have noted from outside. The piers are decorated front and back with simple pilasters and joined by arches to form an arcade which is repeated along the side walls. At the far end of the side aisles are the openings to the 'Lucas' bath and beyond that is a smaller *natatio*. In the 'Lucas' bath room we open one of the doors we noticed at the east end, and we are outside.

It is a simple, but impressive set-up; would we recognise it if we come back a hundred years later? In the main, yes, but we would find considerable changes in detail. In the first place the wooden roof has been replaced by a vault, cunningly constructed in hollow box tiles to keep down the weight (a section of this can be seen in the Baths today), but in spite of this, requiring considerable strengthening of the pillars. The aisles have been given parallel vaults. A new floor has been laid round the Great Bath and the Eastern and Western Baths have been remodelled to provide even better facilities. A Circular Bath has been crammed into the entrance hall and a new room, a *laconium* for intense dry heat, has been built to the west of the main entrance block which has been modified to provide an exercise room, while a new bath has been added to the east of the entrance. There have been other small alterations but these are inconsiderable compared with the complete remodelling of the eastern baths to make a second treatment centre with *tepidarium*, *caldarium* and *apodyterium*; there is also a special semicircular bath in which the patient can sit on steps up to his neck in cold water, a treatment made popular by its use with the Emperor Augustus (23 BC–AD 14) rather in the way Edward VII popularised appendectomy. In fact there were four reconstructions to the east end. We cannot date any of them but various aspects of the changes can be seen today by anyone who visits the Baths. One last change must have come somewhere towards the end of the fourth century when the sea level rose, for in order to combat flooding the hypocausts were filled in throughout the Baths with nine inches of clay, which meant raising the *pilae* and re-making the floors.

In our re-visit we would find changes also in the temple area. The 'dipping-place' has been improved, with better steps and a tidier corner, and the inner precinct has been re-paved, but the biggest alterations are in front of the reservoir enclosure. Here the ground has been raised some 20 inches and re-floored with Pennant sandstone, the local coal-measure sandstone which today floors the Abbey churchyard. This 'high pavement' has done away with the steps to the door of the reservoir and the *stylobate* (pillar-supporting step) of the short colonnade, their place being taken by a free-standing arch.

Of the rest of the city we do not know a great deal. The third building of the central complex, the theatre or forum (or whatever), lay just to the east of the temple precinct and the evidence of masonry found to the north of the Pump Room Hotel suggest another monumental building. Just to the south of the Baths a *stylobate* existed and this indicates yet another unknown building. The location of fragmentary evidence of houses is shown in the map, p. 16 and some mosaics can be seen in the Baths Museum, but three places deserve particular mention.

There are two other major hot springs. They lie west of the Pump Room at the end of Bath Street which was constructed in the 1790s. One is associated with the Cross Bath, the other with the Hot Bath, and both were brought under control in Roman times. The Cross Bath, originally a medieval structure, was rebuilt at the end of the eighteenth century. In 1809, in clearing out the reservoir, there was found an altar dedicated to Sul-Minerva and the Emperor's gods by a centurion of the 2nd Augusta. In the 1880s Major

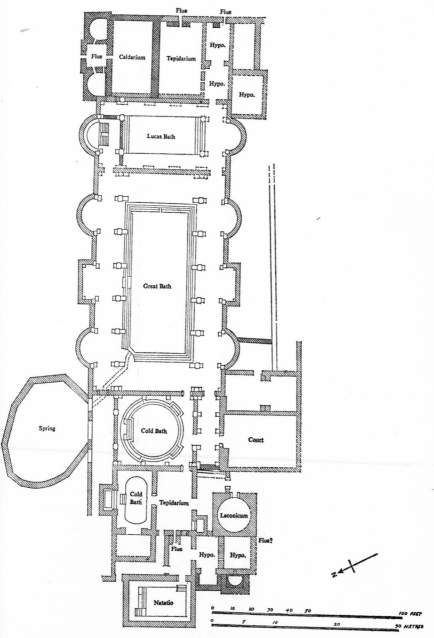

Flue   Flue

Flue   Caldarium   Tepidarium   Hypo.

Hypo.

Hypo.

Lucas Bath

Great Bath

Spring

Cold Bath

Court

Cold
Bath

Tepidarium

Laconicum

Flue?

Flue   Hypo.   Hypo.

Natatio

N

0   10   20   30   40   50   100 FEET
0   5   10   20   50 METRES

The Baths

Davis was at work on the eighteenth-century interior, for which he is castigated by Walter Ison in *The Georgian Buildings of Bath* – 'Only a fragment of this decoration', wrote Ison, 'survived the vandalism of C. E. Davis, who converted this lovely building into a cheap swimming bath during the 1880s' (it was familiarly known as 'the tuppeny hot'). Davis did, however, investigate what he called 'the Roman well' and showed that the diminishing flow reported since the seventeenth century was due to a breakdown in the wall. He also discovered a carved block with themes which may refer to the story Aesculapius, father of medicine. There is no evidence of any Roman temple or baths and it is probable that the reservoir was treated simply as a holy well.

It was otherwise at the Hot Bath. Opposite this, in Beau Street, workmen in 1846 uncovered the foundations of a considerable building with hypocausts, an apsidal room (probably a bath), two other baths, a wall with a pilaster base attached, some flue tiles, and a room 12 by 15 feet with a mosaic ten feet square. They then put the Albert Wing of the Royal United Hospital on top of it. The mosaic was, however, removed and is now in the Baths Museum, flooring a reconstructed Roman room. Whether the remains were of another public bath suite, or a private one, possibly of a hotel or large house, we do not know.

The third location has no known building associated with it. At 'the lower end of Stall Street', were found three altars of which one proclaimed that 'This holy spot, wrecked by insolent hands and cleansed afresh, Gaius Severius Emeritus, centurion in charge of the region, has restored to the Virtue and Deity of the Emperor'. What holy spot? This depends on which is the 'bottom' end of Stall Street – if at the north it could be the temple of Sul-Minerva, if at the south we have an unidentified place of worship. And who wrecked it? Possibly a gang of rowdies (Christian rowdies?), and perhaps the restoration is of the time of Julian the Apostate (Emperor, AD 355–63) who temporarily revoked the decision of

Constantine (AD 305–6) that Christianity was to be the official religion of the Empire.

We have related these finds to Stall Street and a glance at the map would suggest that this was part of the north–south Roman street, crossed by an east–west one perpetuated in Westgate and Cheap Streets, providing the normal *cardo* and *decumanus* of a planned Roman town. It would suggest wrong. The present layout of streets in Bath is the result of eighteenth- and nineteenth-century alterations to the medieval pattern and we have no idea and no indication of how the Roman streets ran; certainly Stall Street, which runs through the site of the temple could not have existed. It may well be that instead of laying out a city pattern and filling in the blocks (*insulae*) with buildings, as was customary, the Romans here started with a group of monumental buildings. The economics of a centre devoted to health, religion, and luxury would then generate a whole complex of ancillary occupations which would need to be housed, many at first in temporary, makeshift buildings.

The temple had attendant priests, augurers, and lesser officials. The precincts needed to be swept, the temple accounts had to be kept, and animals prepared for sacrifice. The number of animals sacrificed during the year was considerable although not on the scale of Rome, where in the celebration of the accession of Caligula over 160,000 were offered up – indeed it is reported that a tipsy Senator, on the occasion of Augustus being away from the city, said that all the bulls and calves must be praying that he never came back. There was doubtless a brisk trade in animals between the local farmers and the visitors and townsfolk.

The building trade was, naturally, important, and there was quite a lot of work for masons in knocking up the numerous little altars and gravestones. The baths needed administrators and a large number of servants such as masseurs, anointers, depilators (for plucking hair from the armpits), perfumers, and cloakroom attendants. A well-to-do Roman needed a lot of attention at the baths – for example, after he had sweated well he was coated with a mixture of oil and sand which was then scraped off with a *strigilis*, a blade of wood or metal. Then there were furnace attendants, feeding the fires with fuel provided by local wood-cutters. Incidentally, it seems probable that the altar fire was fed with coal from local mines, for Solinus, writing his *Collection of Memorable Things* in the third century, mentions 'hot springs in Britain' and that 'over these springs Minerva presides and in her Temple the perpetual fire never whitens into ash but as the flame fades, turns into rocky lumps' – a good description of Somerset coal.

Like any tourist resort today, Roman Bath had a demand for souvenirs but instead of being imported from centres of mass-production, most of them would be made by local craftsmen in little shops or perhaps booths set up around the temple and baths. The carved but unset gems displayed in the Museum indicate that a jeweller was at work in Bath and it is interesting that although many of the tombs and altars are of soldiers there are hardly any military motifs on the gemstones (*intaglios*) in the collection. The stones are mostly cornelian which was probably imported from the Alps and there is further evidence of long-distance imports in the Samian ware (*terra sigillata*) from Gaul. Quite a number of pewter vessels were found but we do not know if there was an industry in Bath; we do know that there was one at the Roman settlement on the Fosse at Camerton six miles south of Bath and stone moulds, probably for pewter vessels, have been dug up on Lansdown. The metal is an amalgam of lead and tin, most likely from the Mendips and Cornwall respectively.

Round about the middle of the second century Aquae Sulis was given an earthen rampart which certainly in part, and most likely throughout, was to be followed by the medieval walls. We can follow the line of the latter today (see map, p. 18). The distance round is about three-quarters of a mile, enclosing an area of 23 acres. If, as seems probable but it not yet proven, a Roman wall was added to the ram-

baths were built by Italians to compensate for being sent to
a cold, wet country. Nor is it at all likely that the native
culture and in particular the native language would have
been completely superseded. It is probable that the villa
owner would talk to his fellow landowners in Latin but to
his farm workers in something akin to Welsh; and that,
while the shopkeeper would bargain with his customer in
the Roman tongue, he would give his assistant orders in the
native speech, possibly larded with Latin words in the sort
of language troops tend to manufacture when they are
stationed in a foreign country.

Direct evidence is confined to epigraphy, that is the
inscriptions on tombs and other monuments. Of these we
have at present 26 of which ten are Army. Of the rest the
only specific occupations mentioned are priest, augurer, a
stonemason, and sculptor. Women and children are repre-
sented by two graves each. There are inscriptions from
troopers, an armourer (who was buried at the expense of his
guild), centurions, freedmen, and people from Gaul and
Spain but the sample is too small for us to make any
generalisation. Were the soldiers on leave, sent for a cure,
or stationed in the vicinity? – we cannot say – nor on the
evidence of six tombs can we say 'They died young' (ages
are 25, 29, 35, 45, 46 and a venerable 80 for a local Senator
decorum from Gloucester). We can, however, say that the
two burial areas found are outside the city and by the main
roads, which is where we would expect them for Roman law
forbade adult burial inside the town. One tomb, however,
was not discovered amongst the others, but to the east of
the town, in Sydney Gardens in 1793. This was of the old
priest, Gaius Calpurnius Receptus, who died at 75. It was
erected by Calpurnia Trifosa 'his freedwoman and wife'. Did
he marry his housekeeper?

3 *Ruin and Reconstruction*
Saxon Times

Despite convulsions in the Empire, reorganisations of governments and army, and attacks from beyond the borders, the fourth century seems to have been a generally prosperous time for much of Britain, and the Bath area was little disturbed. The great combined attack of Picts from Scotland, Scots from Ireland, and Saxons from the North Sea shores in 368 may have led to some destruction at the Kings Weston (Bristol) and Keynsham villas but these recovered. There is some evidence that the defences of the country were weakened by withdrawal of troops, but life must have continued in some comfort. But the light by which they built was that of a setting sun.

In AD 406 the army in Britain decided to join in the game of Emperor-making, and at their third attempt selected Constantine, who immediately sent to the Emperor Honorius explaining that he had been forced into this unwelcome position. The Emperor, however, acknowledged him and he withdrew the bulk of his troops for conquest in Gaul and Spain. Left to themselves the British repudiated him, expelled his officials and in 410 appealed to Honorius for help. But Alaric the Goth was marching on Rome and the Emperor replied that the British must arrange for their own safety as best they could. There is some evidence, subject to considerable controversy by experts, that there was a re-occupation from 417 to 422, but if so it was only a temporary effort. In 446, according to Gildas, who wrote his *De Excidio Britanniae* in the sixth century, a last despairing appeal, 'the groan of the Britons', went unsuccessfully to the Consul Aetius. They had cause to groan; the Saxons were upon them.

It was nearly two hundred years after the legions left Britain that the Saxons took Bath. We have very little idea of what happened round here in the 'long twilight', but it would have been in the nature of a slow strangulation rather than a sudden death. The machinery of government and trade was still in operation and the majority of minor posts of responsibility and the landed estates would be in native hands. What was chiefly lacking was a permanent, highly disciplined military force, a strong central control, and a steady trade. Life on the great estates, the villas such as Keynsham, probably continued much as before but with an increasing emphasis on subsistence farming and a gradual falling-off in the availability of imported goods. The Civil Service continued to function but with gradually waning efficiency while the power of the local nobility grew as the communication system deteriorated. The towns, dependent on trade, communications, administrative functions, a garrison, or, as in the case of Bath, some sort of luxury trade, began to decline.

The towns of the south-west continued longest the trade with the continent, and Bath, situated well to the west of the first Saxon invasions and to the east of the chief Irish attacks, may have avoided for some time any major acts of violence. What is more likely is a general slow decay and depopulation. When the Great Bath was excavated decayed vegetation and a coot's (or teal's?) egg was found in it. On this perhaps rather slender evidence Professor Haverfield wrote: 'The baths disappeared. Their roofs and walls fell in. The hot springs, still forcing their way upwards, formed new pools at a higher level; brushwood and water plants overgrew the debris and marsh-fowl came to nest in the debris.'

Assailed by the Christian Irish (Scots) and the heathen English beleaguered Britain found the latter the more formidable enemy with the most lasting effect. There is some doubt as to their line of advance to the west. The Anglo-Saxon Chronicle, which is not contemporary but was started in the ninth century, attributes the founding of Wessex to the landing of Cerdic and three ships on the coast of Hampshire early in the sixth century. Archaeological and place-name evidence suggests an approach from the Wash along the Icknield Way and the upper Thames valley. It is probable that the first relates to a ruling family, the latter to a mass movement. Whatever the case, our first firm reference to Bath comes from the Anglo-Saxon Chronicle, which says that in 577 'Cuthwine and Ceawlin fought against the Britons and killed three kings, Coinmail, Condidan and Farinmail, at the place which is called Deorham (Dyrham); and they captured three of their cities, Gleawanceaster, Cirenceaster, and Bathanceaster.' This has been taken as implying that Bath was still a going concern as a city but it seems more likely that it is used here as a convenient geographical term, particularly if we consider the evidence of an Anglo-Saxon poem, *The Ruin*, in a volume of English poetry presented to Exeter cathedral in 1050 by Leofric, its first bishop.

This describes a city in ruins and reconstructs its past glories in purely English terms and although it does not name the place it refers specifically to hot baths and could hardly be about anywhere but Bath. '. . . these halls', it says, 'are a dreary ruin, and these pictured gables [presumably the sculptured pediments]; the rafter-framed roof sheddeth its tiles; the pavement is crushed with the ruin, it is broken into heaps . . . there stood the courts of stone. The stream with heat o'erthrew them with its wide burning. Wall all enclosed, with bosom bright, there the baths were, hot on the breast, a comfort indeed!' The Saxon idea of what went on in Bath was rather wide of the mark – 'many the mead-halls, of merriment full . . . many a baron, joyous and gold-bright, splendidly jewelled, haughty and wine-hot, shone in his harness, looked on treasure, on wealth, on curious jewels, on precious stones, on this bright borough of broad dominion'. Indifferent builders themselves, they had a proper respect for the ancient structures – 'the work of giants' they called it and they lamented the passing of such builders – 'Earth's grave holds the mighty workmen, decayed, departed in the hard grip of the grave'.

In 658, according to the Chronicle, eighty-one years after Dyrham, the Saxons beat the British at Peoman (probably Penselwood near Frome) and put them to flight. Bath was now well and truly in Saxon land, but it would appear that in this early period it changed hands from Wessex to the Midland kingdom of Mercia for the first Saxon charter we have is a grant in 675–6 by Osric, king of the Hwiccas and nephew of Wulfhere, king of Mercia of which the Hwiccas formed a sub-kingdom, and entries in the Chronicle would give 628 or 645 as the date of change which was, in a sense, the re-uniting of the old Dobunni area of centuries ago.

The charter, which, like all Saxon charters, is a later copy, appears reasonably authentic. It records the gift of land adjoining the city of Hat Batha to Abbess Bertana for the founding of a nunnery, and it is possible that according to the custom of the time this was a double monastery of monks and nuns. It appears that Aldhelm, founder and abbot of Malmesbury, encouraged the Bath monastery to build a small church to St Michael at the hot springs, but the site is unknown. Aldhelm died in 709 and crosses were erected at the resting place of his coffin from Doulting to Malmesbury, one being at Bath. This may be the one whose fragments are exhibited in the Abbey and which was dug up near the Hot Bath.

What happened to the nunnery we do not know, although the lead cross found at the eastern end of the Baths and inscribed with the name of Eadgyvu may be from the grave of a Saxon princess. An Eadgyvu was grandmother of Edgar who was crowned at Bath in 973, so it is possible that the nunnery was offering board and lodging towards the end of the ninth century. If it continued to exist it was overshadowed by the importance of the monastery of St Peter.

When and by whom St Peter's was founded is not known and the meagre evidence is contradictory. The usual claim is for a founding by Offa, the great Mercian king, in 755, and this is not improbable. The first written date we have is 808, and it is wrong. It is on a charter of Cynewulf, king of the (West) Saxons for a grant of land, confirmed by Offa, to the brethren of St Peter's at Bath. However, the list of witnesses, the confirmation by Offa, and the death of Cynewulf in 786 make this date impossible. The most probable explanation is that the copyist mistook an L for a C and got his date fifty years too late; it would therefore be 758, which is reasonable.

The date of the change of Bath from Mercia back to Wessex is obscure, but hardly important for Ethelflaeda, daughter of Alfred the Great of Wessex, married Ethelred of Mercia and the two kingdoms acted together. When 'The Lady of the Mercians' died in 918, her brother, Edward the Elder, Alfred's successor, claimed lordship over her subjects and from then on English Mercia and Wessex were united. Edward's son Athelstan ruled over Wessex, Mercia, the Danelaw, Cornwall, York, and Northumbria and when he made a land grant to St Peter's in 943–9 he was styled 'King of the English and the peoples around'.

At Athelstan's court was a young monk, born near Glastonbury and nephew to the first bishop of Wells. This monk was Dunstan (ordained in 936). He fell out of favour with the king and his successor, Edmund, but the latter had a change of heart and made Dunstan abbot of Glastonbury. The story has it that Edmund was hunting near Cheddar when his horse bolted for the gorge, at which the king, in desperation, promised the Almighty he would reinstate Dunstan in return for his life. The horse stopped and the king kept his promise. It may have been due to Dunstan's influence that the Bath abbey became Benedictine and received the small influx of foreigners indicated in the *Cartulaire de l'Abbaye de St Bertin* (about 961) which states that in 944 King Edmund gave them refuge at St Peter's, Bath, when they rejected the new strict discipline of the great reformer Gerard de Brogne.

When Edmund was stabbed to death by robbers at Pucklechurch, near Bristol, he was succeeded by his brother, Edred, and then by his nephew, Edwy, who banished Dunstan, reigned for four years, and managed to lose half his kingdom. He did, however, benefit the Bath monastery by restoring one grant of land 'wrongfully taken', and in 957 giving more 'at the petition of the worshipful priest Wulfgar', free of all but the three common dues, the 'trinoda necessitas' of keeping bridges in repair, defending fortresses and serving in war (presumably by financial rather than physical means). This latter charter refers to the 'mira fabrica' of the church.

When Edwy died in 954 the country was reunited under his brother Edgar who appointed Dunstan to the see of Canterbury. In 973 Dunstan consecrated him king at Bath, thirteen years after his accession and two years before his death. The choice of Bath, rather than Kingston-on-Thames is interesting and suggests both that Dunstan had a particular interest in it and that the 'mira fabrica' was indeed impressive. There was no set form of coronation ritual and Dunstan devised one which contained features which have lasted to this day. The Winchester version of the Chronicle recorded in some detail the event at 'the ancient town of Acemanceaster, also called Bath by the inhabitants of this island', in which a 'great congregation of priests, and goodly company of monks and wise men gathered together'. The Peterborough version is more laconic but adds a piece of information of particular interest to Midland readers: 'Soon after this the king led all his fleet to Chester, and there six kings came to him to make their submission and pledged themselves to be his fellow-workers by sea and land.'

This coronation, whose thousandth anniversary is being celebrated in Bath in 1973, lasted long in the memories of the citizens, for as late as the time of Henry VIII the antiquary John Leland recorded that they still held a ceremony at Whitsun and elected one of their number as 'King of Bath', and it was this honorary title which was awarded to Beau Nash in the eighteenth century. With regard to Edgar, the question is why he waited so long. He had probably been crowned before and was undisputed king. Probably it was either considered a good moment to mark his overlordship of England with a splendid ceremony and/or that the consecration was considered most appropriate at the age of 30, which at that time was the earliest that a man could canonically be ordained priest.

In 975 Alphege, who tradition says was born in 953 at Weston by Bath, became abbot of the monastery, and according to *The Golden Legend*, a life of the Saints printed by Caxton, 'bylded ther that fayre abbaye at Bath, and endowed it, and was himself therein fyrst abbot and founder'. This does not fit well with the 'mira fabrica', etc. and probably refers to extensions and improvements. In 984 Alphege became Bishop of Winchester and in 1006 Archbishop of Canterbury where he was martyred by the Danes, who threw bones at him.

By the time of Edward the Confessor the monastery, under its abbot Sewold, was a considerable landowner. Domesday Book records it as possessing most of the manors around Bath, with many mills and well over 1,000 sheep, as well as part of the town with 24 burgesses, a mill, and 12 acres of meadow. These church lands were in 1086 valued at £50 which does not seem much beside some £300 for Glastonbury but is sufficient to argue a modest prosperity. An interesting detail of a more distant land-holding comes from a charter in which the Abbot leased to Archbishop Stigand the manor of Tidenham. This lay on the western fringes of Gloucestershire where the Wye meets the Severn and in Domesday is credited with no fewer than 65 fisheries.

If we have only fragmentary evidence on which to base
our ecclesiastical history of pre-Conquest Bath there is even
less for the secular story. The first dated reference is for 906,
when, according to the Chronicle, 'died Alfred, who was
reeve of Bath'. It is also named in the Burghal Hideage
(918) of Edward the Elder, son of King Alfred. This was a
list of the towns which were to serve as defence centres
against the Danes and to which a tax, or hideage, was to be
paid by the surrounding countryside for maintaining its
fortifications. It was reckoned that 16 hides were needed for
each acre's breadth (Chain) of wall and one man for each
hide, giving four men to each pole of wall. Bath was given
1,000 hides and this would allow for a wall length of about
the same as that in medieval (and probably Roman) times.*
There is no evidence that Bath was called upon to fulfil its
military function and indeed it is unlikely that it would, but
in the troubles with the Danes it does get one mention in
the Chronicle.

During the time of Edgar's son, Ethelred the Unready
(or 'Ill-advised'), the Danish raids had recommenced and,
although he had bought off the attackers with Danegeld,
Ethelred ordered a massacre of the Danes settled in England.
One who died was Gunhilda, sister of Sweyn, King of
Denmark, who invaded with the sworn intention of driving
Ethelred from his kingdom. Landing in 1012, he failed to
force the surrender of London, where Ethelred was, but
then, according to the Chronicle, 'went westward to Bath
and encamped there with his levies. Thither came ealderman
Ethelmaer and the thanes from the went, and they all submitted to Sweyn and gave him hostages, because they were
afraid he would destroy them. Having made his way thus
far, he turned northward to his ships, and the whole nation
accepted him as their undisputed king. Thereafter the
citizens of London submitted and gave hostages.' It is

---

* It has been suggested by P. Greening that there is a margin of 125 yards
between the circuit of the medieval wall of Bath and the hideage figures of
1,375 yards.

possible that the name Swainswick, just outside Bath, derives from this important incident.

We need not concern ourselves here with the death of Sweyn, the return of Ethelred, and the subsequent reigns of Edmund Ironside, Canute, and Edward the Confessor, but it is relevant to note the rise of the Saxon Godwin(e) as Earl of Wessex for it was his daughter Edith who held that part of Bath not held by the Abbey. On her marriage to Edward the Confessor Bath became a Royal borough and when Edward put her into a nunnery and confiscated her estates Bath became a possession of the King. Thus began the split between Royal Bath and Monastic Bath which was to continue, with one short interruption, until the dissolution of the monastery in 1539.

For some detail of the secular city at the end of the Saxon period we must turn to the Norman record, the Domesday Book of 1068. Here we are told that the king had 64 burgesses, paying £4, and that he also had six unoccupied (*vastas*) houses. In late Saxon times, however, people were beginning to invest in town property, and Bath was no exception. Domesday records 90 burgesses 'of other lords', paying a lesser rate of £3. Eight of these belonged to the Manor of Keynsham, one house belonged to 'Hugh the interpreter', and a couple to Edward of Salisbury. If we add in the burgesses of the monastic part and apply the usual multiplier of five (which may be too small) we get a total population of just under 1,000. No market is recorded, nor any mill in the Royal borough, but there was a mint which paid 100s, and its presence implies a certain amount of trade. This should not be exaggerated, for there were six mints mentioned in Somerset, and really important trading places (or *ports*) had several – Athelstan allowed eight to London, seven to Canterbury, and six to Winchester, for example, but by the end of Saxon times there were over twenty at London and over ten at York. In taxation the town paid £60 and one mark of gold, which puts it well below Taunton, which paid £154, but above the other Somerset towns.

Before leaving Saxon Bath we may note one legacy of the period which is still with us – the naming of places. A few names derive from the British tongue, notably Avon (Welsh *Afon*) but the majority come from Old English. If we look at the names of the hills around Bath we have to the north Lansdown (long hill) and Kelston (the calves place) and to the south Odd Down (Odda's hill), Coombe Down (hill of the valley) and Claverton Down (hill above the clover place). Cleft into the southern hills are Widcombe (wide valley) and Lyncombe (valley of the torrent) and ont heir west they descend down Pennyquick (Penna's cow pasture). In surrounding hamlets now incorporated in the city we have Weston (the place west of Bath), Larkhall (lark corner), and Twerton (or Twiverton – two-ford), and to the north lies Charlecombe (the valley of the churls or carls – free peasants). Also in the city, but just north of the city wall lies the parish of Walcot. Now the Saxon name for the British was *wealas*, or 'foreigners', which seems a rather presumptuous title for invading aliens to give to the native population. *Wealas* became Welsh, and Walcot can be taken to mean 'the dwelling of the Welsh', a surburban community of native Britons established just outside the Saxon city.

Interpretation of place names is fraught with difficulties and obvious explanations are not always correct. An example in Bath is Bear Flat. The meaning seems obvious and there is a Bear Hotel with an effigy of the appropriate animal, but if we look at early documents we find that the name was once Berewick. *Bere* in Old English means 'barley' (hence 'beer') and *wick* has a number of associated meanings, one of which is 'farm'. Bear Flat was therefore originally 'barley farm': then the wick got lost, the *bere* became *bear*, and 'flat' was tacked on as describing the physical nature of the place. *Bere* also enters into 'Barton' which came to mean an outlying farm or grange. North-west of the walls there was such a farm in medieval times and its name is perpetuated in Barton Street.

One local name which would appear Roman is in fact

medieval Latin and refers to an area of legal administration introduced in the late Saxon period. This is the name Bath Forum. Forum is an abbreviation of *forinsecum* and is the area adjacent to Bath in the north forming the nucleus of the Hundred of Bath Forum.

4 Monks and Merchants

The Middle Ages

The year after the Domesday inquest the Conqueror died, and his realm was split between his sons. Robert, the elder, got Normandy, and William, nicknamed Rufus because of his red face, succeeded to England. As a result, reported the Chronicle, 'there was great commotion in this country and treason was everywhere'. The rebellion against Rufus was led by three fighting bishops, Odo of Bayeux, Geoffrey of Coutances, who was a considerable landholder in Somerset, and Hugh of Durham. It took place mainly in the east, with much devastation, and quickly failed, but the little there was in Somerset was disastrous to Bath, a Royal borough, for Bishop Geoffrey and his nephew, Robert Mowbray, made the strong castle at Bristol their centre from which 'they sallied forth . . . and ravaged Bath and all the surrounding countryside'.

The following year, 1088, Bishop Giso of Wells died and Rufus gave the see to his physician, John de Villula, otherwise known as John of Tours, with the stipulation that he moved its seat to Bath. This was in accordance with a decree in 1075 of the Council of London that bishops' seats should be moved as soon as possible from small towns and villages to more populous places and the choice of Bath could suggest that the place, though ravaged, was by no means desolate. On the other hand this may have been a move designed to

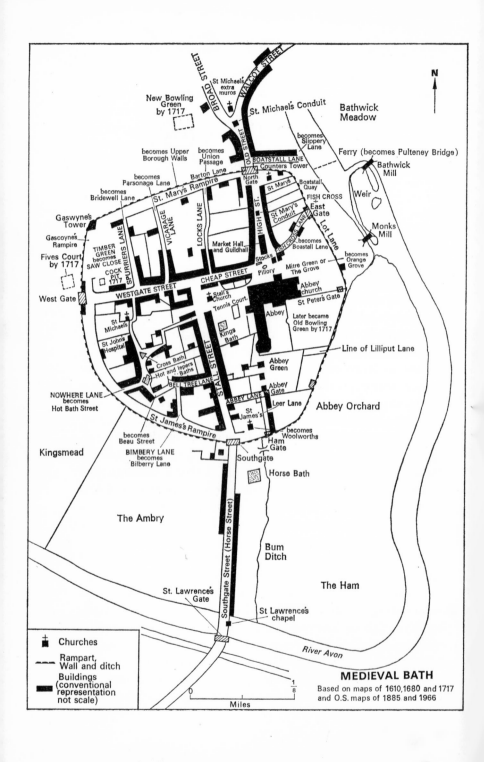

MEDIEVAL BATH

Based on maps of 1610, 1680 and 1717 and O.S. maps of 1885 and 1966

N

St Michaels extra muros

New Bowling Green by 1717

St. Michael's Conduit

Bathwick Meadow

BROAD STREET

WALCOT STREET

becomes Slippery Lane

Ferry (becomes Pulteney Bridge)

Bathwick Mill

becomes Upper Borough Walls

becomes Union Passage

BOATSTALL LANE
Counters Tower

Boatstall Quay

Weir

OLD STREET

Barton Lane

North Gate

St Marys

FISH CROSS
East Gate

becomes Parsonage Lane

St. Mary's Rampire

St Mary's Conduit

Monks Mill

becomes Bridewell Lane

LOCKS LANE

HIGH ST.

FISH CROSS LANE

Lot Lane

Gaswyne's Tower

VICARAGE LANE

becomes Boatstall Lane

becomes Orange Grove

Gascoynes Rampire

Market Hall and Guildhall

Mitre Green or The Grove

Fives Court by 1717

SPURRIERS LANE

TIMBER GREEN becomes SAW CLOSE

Stocks
Pillory

Abbey church

West Gate

COCK PIT 1717

CHEAP STREET

St Peters Gate

WESTGATE STREET

Stall's Church

Abbey

Later became Old Bowling Green by 1717

Tennis Court

St Michaels

Kings Bath

Line of Lilliput Lane

St Johns Hospital

Abbey Green

Cross Bath
Hot and lepers Baths

STALL STREET

BELL TREE LANE

Abbey Gate

NOWHERE LANE becomes Hot Bath Street

ABBEY LANE

St James's

Leer Lane

Abbey Orchard

St James's Rampire

becomes Beau Street

Ham Gate

becomes Woolworths

Kingsmead

BIMBERY LANE becomes Bilberry Lane

Southgate

Horse Bath

The Ambry

Southgate Street (Horse Street)

Bum Ditch

The Ham

St. Lawrence's Gate

St Lawrence's chapel

River Avon

Churches

Rampart, Wall and ditch

Buildings (conventional representation not scale)

0 ⅛

Miles

rehabilitate a shattered city. Certainly John of Tours started on a building programme, notably of a great new cathedral to replace the old Abbey church and a palace (the 'bysschepesbour' – Bishop's Bower).

Later bishops preferred to live at Wells and the Bower fell into disrepair; when Leland visited in the sixteenth century he wrote 'only one gret square Tour of it with other Ruines yet appere'. The Norman church was an impressive edifice, but only a few scraps remain, exhibited in the present cloisters, and one arch, with one column on its left side, at the east end of the south chancel aisle. The church was some 354 feet (108 metres) long and extended far beyond the east end of the present Abbey which stands on the Norman nave. John did not see it completed but building continued under his successors and although it was attacked by fire in July 1137 it was subsequently repaired by Bishop Robert. Later, however, it became very dilapidated for the bishops seem to have lost interest in Bath and transferred their attentions to Wells, until Bishop King took in hand the building of the present church in about 1500.

To the medieval inhabitants of Bath the Abbey was not just a church but an organisation with a whole complex of buildings (dormitories, workshops, dining room, kitchens, school offices, etc.), set in gardens and orchards, surrounded by its own walls and gates, stretching southward from the church of St Peter, and occupying nearly a quarter of the town (see map). Nothing of this now remains except for a hinge, reputedly from the Abbey gate, set in a wall to the south of Abbey Green, but recent excavations have proved the precinct wall in two places. One in Abbeygate Street revealed what was probably the foundation of the gate, and the other, near Woolworth's, showed the Ham Gate which led from the precinct to the fields by the river. Properly speaking we should not refer to an Abbey at Bath, for when it became the bishop's seat (or *cathedra*) the bishop became nominally abbot and the working head of the monastery was demoted to prior. Thus the monastery became a priory and

St Peter's a priory church; however, custom has preserved the name of Abbey and we will continue to use it.

As a physician it is likely that John of Tours took a particular interest in promoting Bath as a centre of healing, for which it soon became famous. In the *Gesta Stephani* (twelfth century), we read that 'sick persons from all over England go there to bathe in the healing waters, as well as the healthy, who go to see the wonderful outpourings of water and bathe in them'. If, as is possible, this was written by Robert de Lewes, Bishop of Bath, some allowance may be made for partisanship, but this would not apply to Alexander Necham the twelfth-century canon of St Albans who wrote in his Latin verses *In praise of Divine Wisdom*:

Our baths at Bath with Virgil's to compare,
For their effects, I dare almost be bold,
For feeble folk, and sickly, good they are,
For bruised, consumed, far spent, and very old,
For those likewise whose sickness comes of cold.

These baths, the King's, Cross, and Hot, were under the jurisdiction of the Bishop, and were administered by the Prior. It seems that John of Tours also built two baths in the monastery, the Abbot's (public) and the Prior's (private), fed from the King's Bath for Leland wrote: 'Ther goith a sluse out of this (King's bath) and servid in Tymes past with Water derivid out of it 2 places in Bath Priorie used for Bathes: els voide: for in them be no springs.' It is unlikely that the monks had much personal use for the baths, for the Benedictine rule classified bathing with flesh-eating as suitable only for the sick, the young, the aged, and the guests.

Although the Priory collected quite a useful library it was never a renowned seat of learning. It may, however, have given early training to the famous Adelard of Bath who, after studying at Tours, travelled widely in Europe and the Middle East and was important for translating Euclid and Ptolemy (the astronomer) from Arabic versions. He was

back in England between 1142 and 1144, writing a treatise
on the astrolabe, and very possibly at Bath for the book is
dedicated to the young Henry Plantagenet who was then at
Bristol.

John de Villula had also acquired the Royal Borough and,
with commendable caution, ensured that the transaction
was agreed by Robert of Normandy. He paid the rather
large sum of £500 which led to some contemporary insinua-
tions that this was part of a deal over the appointment to
the see. It is possible; as we shall see later the town figured
in two more transactions, one when bishop Savaric gave it
back to the Crown in exchange for the Abbey of Glastonbury, the other when Edward 1 handed it back to the bishop
in exchange for the patronage of Glastonbury.

In December 1122 John de Villula died and was buried
before the altar of his church. 'His image', wrote Leland,
'I saw lying there an 9 Yere sins, at the which tyme al the
Church that he made lay to waste, and was onrofid, and
wedes grew about this John of Tours Sepulchre.' He was
succeeded by the Queen's chaplain, Godfrey, who was
followed in 1136 by Robert of Lewes, the first appointment
made by King Stephen. Henry had left the crown to his
daughter Matilda, wife of Geoffrey Plantagenet and
Stephen, who was grandson of the Conqueror, had sworn
fealty to her. The temptation, however, was too much and
he had seized the throne, 'trusting', as a contemporary
account by the Archdeacon of Huntingdon said, 'in his
strength'. Civil war and anarchy ensued. 'Christ', said the
Chronicle, 'and His angels slept.' The Bishop was in Bath,
which was being held for the King, when one of the leaders
of the Queen's party, Geoffrey Talbot was discovered there
in disguise and was imprisoned. In return a party from
Bristol came over at midnight and kidnapped the Bishop.
After appropriate negotiation the two prisoners were exchanged. Stephen was furious, partly because Talbot was
more use to him than Robert, partly because he suspected
the Bishop of connivance. As a result he imprisoned Robert

himself – but only for a while. The whole unhappy Stephen/
Matilda business was settled when her son, the future
Henry II, came over from France and was acknowledged by
Stephen as his heir. 'Thus, by God's mercy', wrote the
Archdeacon, giving credit where it was due, 'he contrived
to bring to a close the gloomy night that had disturbed the
sacred realm of England and to herald the dawn of peace.'
And peace indeed settled about, if not inside, the city and
priory of Bath.

Three main themes run through the story of Bath in the
Middle Ages – the continuing use of the baths, the ups,
downs, and dissensions of the Priory, and the development
of the City as a commercial centre. The baths we will deal
with in the next chapter, and as we have so far had much to
say about the Priory we will continue its story before dis-
cussing the town.

Bishop Robert, recovered from the wrath of Stephen, was
another builder of Bath, erecting a chapter-house, cloister,
dormitory, refectory, infirmary, and other buildings for the
monks. He also got the Pope to acknowledge formally in
1157 that Bath was the seat of the bishopric. In 1166 he
died and the see was vacant for seven years, during which
time, about 1170, the Bishop of Llandaff visited Bath, at the
invitation of the Prior to dedicate a chapel to a trio of saints
– Werburga, John the Evangelist, and Katherine; Werburga was a Mercian princess who became head of all the
nunneries in that kingdom and her rather limited cult
probably dates from a Norman foundation at Chester.

The next bishop, Reginald FitzJocelin (1174–91)
founded in his first year the Hospital of St John by the
Cross Bath and gave it to the Priory in 1180; the present
Hospital is on the same site but is an eighteenth-century
building by John Wood with recent alterations. He also
endowed the monastery with many gifts of relics, ornaments,
vestments, and books, and gave them permission to appropriate the church at Bathford for the maintenance of the
church fabric and assigned the Whitsuntide offerings of the

diocese to rebuilding it. It was Reginald who, with the Bishop
of Durham, was the first bishop to 'support' a monarch,
Richard I, at his coronation, a privilege enjoyed to this day.
Elected to the see of Canterbury, he died on the journey
there.

He was succeeded by Savaric, Archdeacon of Northamp-
ton, a Burgundian and a relative of the Emperor Henry VI,
with whom he had negotiated the ransom of Richard I,
demanding the see of Bath as a reward. An ambitious man,
he would not brook the virtual independence within his see
of the great monastery of Glastonbury. With the backing of
the King he had himself made Abbot of Glastonbury, moved
his *cathedra* there, and was styled Bishop of Bath and
Glastonbury. In return he gave the borough of Bath back
to the Crown. He did not entirely neglect the Priory for he
gave it grants of land and paid its contributions to Richard's
ransom out of the revenues of the see. During his time
certain Irish monasteries – Waterford, Youghal, and Cork
– placed themselves under Bath. This was not appreciated
as they were poor and their lands hardly paid for their own
upkeep.

Glastonbury did not relinquish the struggle and in 1219
the next bishop, Jocelin, was persuaded to give up the
abbacy in exchange for various manors in Somerset; he did,
however, retain the patronage. During the reign of King
John the Bishop was banished abroad from 1208 to 1213
and in this time the Priory suffered three unhappy visits
from the King in 1209, 1212, and 1213, and in the last
year the monks were forced to make a free grant of all the
King had taken from them for his court. This left them so
hard up that they had to borrow from Canon Ralph de
Lechlade of Wells to buy themselves corn.

Jocelin's death in 1242 brought the matter of election to
a head. Bath chose Roger of Salisbury, and Wells appealed
to Rome, who condemned the election but confirmed the
appointment. The next year the Pope, in a letter from
Lyons, settled the matter. There were in future to be joint

elections, the installation was to be in both churches, and the title was to be Bishop of Bath and Wells (Episcopus Bathoniensis at Wellensis). The title remains but the dissolution of Bath Priory removed the double election.

The next Bishop was the worldly Burnell, Chancellor to Edward I who named one of his bastide towns in Gascony Bath after Burnell's title but was unsuccessful in his attempt to secure Canterbury for him. Glastonbury was still struggling to be free of the Bishop and in 1275 Edward took over the patronage himself, compensating the Bishop with a fine of 1,000 marks on Glastonbury, a rent charge on the manor of Congresbury, and the gift of 'our city of Bath and its suburbs, together with our houses, gardens, and meadows, and the advowsons of the churches of the said city, together with all fines, amerciaments, and tallages . . . except the Berton of Bath, which the Prior and Convent of Bath hold in fee-farm'. In order to make this gift he had to take it away from Queen Eleanor to whom he had previously presented it but he gave her Rye in exchange! Later the King tried to get a £30 yearly rent for the city out of the Prior, who pointed out that when Savaric handed Bath to the Crown the Prior had been made free of this. Edward himself visited Bath in 1276 and 1285 and it is possibly as a result of these visits that there was an inquisition when the jury found the Prior had pulled down a building on the city wall to get materials for the monastery, and had failed to keep the King's bath and lodgings in repair.

The priors do not seem to have been, on the whole, very outstanding men and the history of the Priory is one of recurring financial trouble and occasional moral slackness which engaged the attention of successive bishops. Robert de Clopecote (1301–32) was particularly extravagant and all Bishop Drokensford's attempts to get at the truth appear to have been met with a conspiracy of silence. He had ideas above his station and in 1321 petitioned the Pope to be allowed to wear insignia like a 'mitred abbot'. The Pope refused, saying it would be 'non congruente'. His successor,

Thomas Crist, could only stand the job for eight years and then retired on a pension, to be followed by Ford who not only borrowed large sums of money and provided for friends and relatives out of Priory funds, but had a mistress in one of the Priory manors in Gloucestershire. In spite of some anxious correspondence between the two bishops concerned Ford does not seem to have been dismissed. The crimes of Prior Sir Thomas Lacock ('Sir' was a courtesy title for a priest) are not known, but the Bishop ordered a court to be held 'in Bath Cathedral' in 1452 to hear his purgation and his purgators. Purgation was the affirmation on oath by the accused in a spiritual court that he was innocent, confirmed by the oaths of several of his peers, a less painful process than 'vulgar purgation' more commonly known as trial by ordeal.

It might be a lack of forceful priors which led to the absence of the usual record of strife so often found where monks and citizens shared a town. The only discord we hear of has a somewhat farcical touch. This was the Battle of the Bells, which broke out in 1408, appeared to be settled, and was then revived by the Mayor, Richard Widcombe, in 1417. The Prior claimed the right for Le Clock, his bell in St Mary of Stalls on the corner of Stall and Cheap streets, to be the first and last to ring each day. This the Mayor denied and proclaimed independence by having the other church bells rung 'outside hours'. The noisy quarrel dragged on for years, even after Widcombe had appealed to Henry v and been told to 'cesse of al such manere newe and wilfulle gouvernaunce', and it was not until 1423 that Bishop Bubwith settled this campanological contest with a masterly compromise. Time was to be taken from Le Clock but 'knollynges' and 'tyllynges' were allowed between midnight and when Le Clock struck six in the morning and there were other portionings out of time. Le Clock was to be rung by a man who took his oath of office to the Prior, but was appointed by the citizens. The use of bells for time-keeping was of course important but people of Bath, especially the sick, might well welcome some curb on 'knollynges', 'tyllynges', and 'peeles'. Indeed, in the eighteenth century there was a quite strong anti-bell movement.

Although in general the fabric of the church was neglected, in 1335 a restoration was done, with a decree from Edward III that a general collection for expenses should be held throughout the diocese. In recognition, statues of Edward, of Bishop Ralph, and of Prior John de Berewyk were placed on the south gate. Another Prior, Cantlow, built a leper hospital and church of St Mary Magdelen on the Holloway, outside the city, and this church, although enlarged in 1823 and again after the war, still contains some of the oldest architecture in Bath, notably in the south porch.

In 1495 Oliver King, one-time scholar of Eton, Fellow of King's, Canon of Windsor, in whose St George's chapel he is buried, and trusted servant of Henry VII, was elected Bishop of Bath and Wells. In 1499, just before the death of Prior Cantlow, he visited Bath and did not like what he saw. Feasting he found, and idleness, women too often present, and at unseemly hours, and the church grievously dilapidated. He therefore gave instructions for strict dining rules, with no meat except for the physically weak, strict clothing rules, and the return to store of all possessions which were not absolutely necessary. For rebuilding the ruinous church he set aside £300 out of a yearly revenue of £480 and entrusted the work to Prior Birde, whom he appointed, quashing the convent's election which had taken place without his licence. According to Sir John Harington, whom we shall meet again, the Bishop's building was inspired by 'a vision of the Holy Trynitie, with angels ascending and descending by a ladder, neer to the foote of which there was a fayre Olive tree, supporting a crown, and a voice that said – 'Let an OLIVE establishe the Crowne, and let a KING restore the Churche''.' 'At the west end', wrote Harington, 'he caused a representation of the Trynities, the angells, and the ladder; and on the north side the olive and crown', and these can be seen, much restored, today,

9 Charter of Richard I

10 The city centre, showing the Abbey and surrounding area (photograph taken in 1930s)

together with a Victorian statue of Henry VII over the main doorway.

The Bishop took a personal interest in the new church and employed the King's masons, William and Robert Vertue, for the design. In a letter, 'At my monastery of Bathe foresaid in the xviij day of Janyver with the scribbling hand of hym that ys all your owne Oliver Bathe', written to Sir Reginald Bray, who was in general charge of the King's works, the Bishop says that the Vertues have been with him and have promised him a vault for the chancel 'whereunto they say nowe ther shal be noone so goodely neither in england nor in france'; he also enquires what bargain his agent at Southampton has made for the hundred cases of glass from Normandy. A week later he is writing about labour troubles. Apparently some of the men wanted to knock off for a month, until Candlemas, to do 'other mennys businesses' and he asks Sir Reginald not to give them licence; he is particularly anxious to keep Thomas Lynn, who was appointed by Robert Vertue.

It was decided to pull down what was left of the old Norman church and build a smaller one in its place, using the old pillar foundations of the nave. The result is that, although the building suffered greatly after the Dissolution and there has been much renovation, we have in Bath the last great church in England built in a contemporary Perpendicular style, that final flowering of the Gothic which is particular to England. It is a soaring style which combines lightness with strength and dignity and, as its name suggests, has a strong accent on vertical lines, particularly in the window tracery. Arches are flatter than in previous styles and are usually four-centred, that is each side is made up of two arcs, each with a different radius and therefore a different curve. The use of wall tracery which is often a feature of the Perpendicular, as at Gloucester, is not much in evidence at Bath apart from the beautiful carving on Prior Birde's chantry, but fan vaulting, an English invention of the fourteenth century, is a striking feature of the Abbey's

interior. In keeping with the rest of the church it is restrained
and dignified in form. It is not, in fact, all original, for the
nave was never completed in the first building and was later,
as we shall see, given a Jacobean timber roof; its fan vaulting
is Victorian – and none the worse for it.

Oliver King died in 1540, and the vaulting bears the
arms of his successor, Adrian di Castello, an absentee bishop
who spent much of his time at the court of the Borgia Pope.
Prior Birde died in 1525 and is commemorated in his
chapel, already mentioned, which was begun in 1515.
Building was continued by his successor, William Hollewey,
otherwise known as Gibbs (1525–39), Bath's last prior,
who did not have time to complete it before the dissolution.
The document recording his election gives the number of
monks as 21, probably the largest number since the Great
Plague, the Black Death of 1349, reduced them from 40 to
18 (approximately). The end of the monastery we will consider in the next chapter; for the moment we will step back
to consider the civil history of medieval Bath.

As was often the case in towns, an early administration
came into being in answer to the needs of a growing mercan-
tile community and expressed itself in the form of merchant
guilds. As this developed the citizens (who were by no
means the whole population) would wish to have their
powers and authority backed by the King and to establish
their autonomy, particularly in the matters of local taxation
and law. In other words, they would seek a Charter.

Such charters were often obtained when the King was in
need of money. Thus the first Bath charter was granted by
Richard I on 7 December 1189 at Dover, only four days
before he set sail for the expensive First Crusade, and refers
not to government but to trade. The merchant guild was to
have all the privileges already given to Winchester, that is
a freedom from all tolls and customs, by land and sea, for
their goods, and a £10 fine for anyone who interfered with
these rights.

These valuable, though usual, privileges, did not

strengthen the hands of the citizens within the town, and so a further charter was sought. In this the Crown surrendered the right to seize personal estates of deceased persons, and gave the citizens the right to elect coroners and execute writs 'so that no sheriff or other bailiff or officer of ours shall intrude himself in the matter of summonses in the said City'. So, although the Crown left an escape clause, the city had taken an important step forward in self government, or rather government by a group of its own citizens.

We know of this charter only from a ratifying *inspeximus* of Edward II in 1313. The curious thing is that although the *inspeximus* says the original charter was given by Henry III on 24 July 1256 the only one known of that date refers simply to exemption of citizens from arrest for debt in certain circumstances. This suggests that either there is a 'lost charter' of exactly the same date, or that the citizens fooled the Crown into ratifying a forgery, both unlikely explanations.

A charter, of Henry VI in 1447, refers to a Mayor and gives him important judicial powers. He is to be *Custos Pacis* and shall enquire of felonies and other offences, for the citizens shall not be called to answer at the County Sessions for things arising out of offences in the city and no other justices shall intrude themselves into the city. The Mayor is also given the assay and assize (that is Assessment and price regulation) of bread, wine, beer, and other kinds of victuals and saleable goods, and correction of weights and measures, and the King's clerk of the market is not to enter. These concessions were not, however, to prejudice the powers of the Bishop. Much of the charter refers to market regulations and the citizens already had right, by an earlier charter of Edward III, of exemption from certain market dues which would be charged on anyone from outside. These were charges for murage (wall-making), stallage (erecting market stalls), panage (feeding swine in woodland), and piccage (breaking up ground for setting up stalls).

The market, which was held in the High Street, was the

means of bringing together town and country products for the locality. Of much wider influence was the annual fair, and the right to hold such an event was an important one. The first one was granted to the Bishop by the Pope in 1156, 'with pleas, laws, judgements and customs, markets, tolls and fairs on either feast of St Peter' and this was confirmed by a bull of 1178 'as freely as king William II and king Henry I held the same, as they were granted to Bishop John (of Tours)'. This implies a Royal Charter but none is recorded until 1284 when Edward I empowered Bishop Robert to hold a fair on the vigil, feast, and morrow of SS Peter and Paul and 7 days following; the feast was on 29 June, but after the New Style calendar was introduced in 1752, advancing dates by 11 days, the date changed to 10 July. In the *Traveller's Pocket Book* of 1785 it is described as a cattle fair but was known later as Cherry Fair and lasted until 1851, being held in the High Street and adjoining streets.

The Prior was granted a fair much later, in 1304, for the vigil and feast of St Lawrence the Martyr (10 August), extended in 1335 by Edward III to six days. It was held in the Barton, outside the city, and continued longer than the monastery for it is mentioned in 1792 but seems to have ceased by 1801. The Prior was also given one on the Priory estates to the south of the river and this was still held when Collinson was writing his *History of Somerset* in 1795. He says that it was held on 4 May and was called Holloway Fair.

The Mayor seems to have had to wait much longer. There is indirect evidence in a complaint of 1275 that Henry III had granted a fair to the Prior of Hinton (Hinton Charterhouse, five miles south of Bath) on the Beheading of John the Baptist (29 August) which clashed with one which 'the King was accustomed to hold in the City of Bath' and caused 'damage to the City of Bath of 10s per annum'. As there is no later mention of this Bath fair it would seem that the competition may well have killed it. In any case there is no further record until the time of Henry VIII when in 1544 the City was granted a fair for 1 February and six following days, with a Court of Piepoudre (*Curia Pedis Pulverizati*) and all tolls, purprestres, etc. The Piepoudre ('dusty-foot') Court was a special one for a fair, set up to deal summarily with the misdoings of wayfarers and travelling traders, while purprestre was a tax on setting up booths, although it originally referred to the encroachment of buildings on forest land. The fair was held until 1854 when it was curtailed to a cattle fair. It came to be known as the Orange Fair and was held in Walcot Street, outside the old city walls, on 2 February, the Feast of the Purification.

The notable Lansdown Fair, on the high hill to the north of Bath, was not medieval but was granted by Queen Anne in a charter of 1708. It was a livestock fair and was for 11 and 12 August although later it ran for three days from the 10th. It continued as a one-day fair until about the middle of the nineteenth century and we have a vivid description of it in 1848 by Lord George Sanger in his book *Seventy Years a Showman*. It is worth leaping out of time-context to consider his remarks. At that time, he says, Bath had in its slums 'what was considered to be the most brutish and criminal mob in England, and for these people Lansdowne Fair was, as they put it, their night out'. After the regular business was finished and the dealers had left, this mob descended in the deepening dusk upon the fair. 'The scenes that followed', says Sanger, 'were almost indescribable. Not content with drinking all they could, the ruffians staved in barrels, turned on taps, and let the liquor run to waste. Then they started to wreck the booths. Canvas was torn to shreds, platforms were smashed up and made bonfires of, wagons were battered and overturned, show-fronts that had cost some of their owners small fortunes were battered to fragments. Everywhere was riot, ruin, and destruction.' Hooliganism isn't what it used to be!

To return to the charters. They did not grant privileges to all the inhabitants of the city but to the 'citizens', or freemen, and it seems that this status could be acquired either by seven years' apprenticeship or by purchase. The Freeman's Oath of 1412 preserved in the *Red Book of Bath*, a vellum manuscript now at Longleat, shows that the chief duty of a freeman was to preserve the privileges of other freemen.

I schal buxom [docile] and obedyant be to the mayr of bathe and to al hys successorys and I schal mentayne me [attach myself] to no lordyshyp for hynderans of any burges of bath. Nether I schal nozth plete with [bring any suit against] no burges of bathe but on the mayr court yf hit so be that the mayr will do me ryght or may do me ryght [if the mayor is willing and competent]. Seynt Katern day I schal kepe holy day yerely and Seynt Katern Chapell [in St Mary-le-Stall] and the brygge [bridge] help to mentayne and to susteyn by my powre. All other customys and Fredumys that longit to the fore sayde fredom I schal well and truly kepe and mentayne on my behalfe selove God and halydome [so help me God and his holy angels].

The business activities of the freemen and other people of the town are very poorly documented and much will have to be inferred from knowledge of other places. In general the medieval town received its income from three sources – agriculture, manufacture, and trade – along with the ancillary service occupations such as the provision of hospitality and entertainment. These are all interrelated (for example, sheep-rearing and woollen manufacture) but for simplicity we will look briefly at each in turn.

Not only was a town well supplied with gardens and orchards within its walls, as can be seen in maps of Bath as late as the seventeenth century, not only did it have a considerable animal population, especially of pigs, but townspeople also had rights in the land outside both for arable, and more particularly for pasture. Most of the land adjacent to the city was held by the Prior, and the *Nomina Villarum* of 1315–16 shows him as having the Barton, Weston,

Batheaston, Bathford, Walcot, Lyncombe, Widcombe, and South Stoke (see map, p. 44), while Kelston was held by the Abbess of Shaftesbury, Bathwick and Woolley by the Abbess of Wherwell, and Swainswick by John Hese. An *inspeximus* of 1279 confirms that the Bishop had extended the Priory lands by granting the land between the city wall and the Avon on the south and east from the bridge round to the monks' mill. The southern pasture (and in the seventeenth century the town rubbish-dump) was called the Ham, for access to which the Priory was empowered to make a new gate in the wall (the Ham gate) 'for carrying their hay and driving their beasts in fair time to the pasture'.

Much of the farmland would have been in great open fields, and we have a thirteenth-century grant of land in Lyncombe of acres and half acres located within the lower and upper fields which suggests their division into the customary strips. On the other hand a gradual process of consolidation and enclosure was taking place; a medieval document specifically mentions certain enclosures in Lyncombe, including a vineyard, a park, a bee-croft, and gives permission for more land to be separated from the common fields. It is probable that some citizens would have arable strips and there is definite evidence that they had the right of common, that is to turn their animals out into the Prior's land in Bath Forum. We know of this because there were disputes about it in the seventeenth and eighteenth centuries in which references to ancient practices were quoted.

It seems that the Barton was divided into three main areas, the meadows (i.e. land which was mown for hay) of Kingsmead, a pasture called West field, and an arable area, the Barton farm. The citizens, or 'freemen', had the right to turn out their cattle on to Kingsmead at Lammas ('loaf-mass' – 1 August) and on the Barton arable three weeks after the farmer had turned out his; for this they paid 1d for each toothed beast and ½d for each untoothed (e.g. geese and old sheep). This became extremely inconvenient to the Barton farmer and a long period of litigation at the end of the fifteenth century with one, Sir George Snigge, resulted in a settlement by Sir Nicholas Hyde, Recorder of Bath, in which rights of common were concentrated in the West field with the proviso that 'the same lands or part thereof be not at any time converted to the private profit of any in particular, but of the burgesses in general'. This proviso gave rise to two more bouts of litigation, one in 1791 when the commoners complained that the mayor and corporation had not been sharing out the profits (for right of common had been converted into rent) and another in the eighteenth century when some of the commoners wanted to sell off the land for building. The Commons remain to this day, contributing to the health rather than the economy of the citizens, being part golf course, part park, and part allotments.

The manufactures of the town would in part be concerned with the production of local consumer goods and would concentrate in their own areas, as witness Spurriers Lane (now Bridewell Lane), but the most important trade would probably be in woollen cloth. Leland wrote that 'The Toun hath of a long tyme syns bene continually most mayntainid by making of Clothe' and adds, 'There were in hominum memoria 3 Clotheirs at one tyme, thus namid Style, Kent, and Chapman, by whom the Toun of Bath then flourished. Syns the Death of them it hath sumwhat decayed' – a decline borne out by the Mayor in 1622 who wrote: 'We are a verie little poore Citie, our Clothmen much decayed, and many of their workmen amongst us relieved by the Citie.'

The most famous reference to a local cloth industry is in *The Canterbury Tales:*

A good Wyf was ther of bisyde Bathe,
But she was som-del deef, and that was scathe.
Of cloth-making she hadde swich an haunt,
She passed hem of ypres and of gaunt.

'Bisyde Bathe' may very well refer to Twerton where cloth-making continued down to the present century. Other evidence comes from names on a Poll Tax Roll of 1340 – Henry le Webber, Thomas le Touker (a tucker was a fuller), Ralph le Taylour, Walter le Lindraper, and Nicholas le Chaloner (blanket-maker) – and a Subsidy Roll of 1379 which mentions dyers, fullers, webbers, and filators, while the importance of the industry may be deduced from the fact that in the fourteenth century MPs for Bath included three weavers, a cloth maker, a cloth merchant and a chapman. Apart from the citizens, the Priory was much concerned with the cloth trade and incorporated a shuttle in its coat of arms. There are records of the Prior ordering 300 sacks of wool from Malmesbury in 1334 and 600 sacks three years later, and a charter of Edward III in 1371 confirms that the two markets a week on Wednesdays and Saturdays which the Prior had held 'from time immemorial' was 'as well for woollen cloth as for other merchandise and saleable goods of whatsoever kind'. Incidentally, Edward extended the market, which had been from the Feast of Pope Calixtus (14 October) to Palm Sunday, to the whole year.

It is not surprising that Bath, with its nearby sheep-pastures, its fuller's earth in the hills above, its river for water and power, and its proximity to a great port, should have developed a woollen industry, but it is difficult to account for the early decline. Bath had ceased to be important for wool long before towns such as Frome, Bridgwater, Taunton, or Stroud, and it is possible that in spite of the Wife of Bath it had not been particularly important for the trade. Town industry tended to decline in the later Middle Ages as the capitalists began to put work out into the country where they were not restricted by guild regulations; complaints went to the government from several towns in Somerset, but not, apparently, from Bath. Dissolution of the Priory may have adversely affected industry, but the decline was noted before this event. Nor can we put it down to rival employment, for Bath had not yet become a fashionable pleasure centre, and the many people who came to the baths did not bring much revenue, even when augmented by the method complained of by Bishop Bubwith in 1449, that when the bathers

> through modesty and shame try to cover their privy parts, the men with drawers and the women with smocks, they, the said people, barbarously and shamelessly strip them of the said garments and reveal them to the gaze of the bystanders, and inflict on them not only the loss of their garments but a heavy monetary fine.

It may well be, therefore, that we should look to particular and personal causes, and that the decay of the cloth industry in Bath may have been due, as Leland suggested, to the loss of three of its leading figures.

With regard to trade, we have already mentioned the fairs and markets, and several leases refer to shops and taverns. We could go further and describe the crowd on a fair day on Barton Fields with stalls selling West Country cloths like Bath Beaver, Cary cloths, plunkets, and narrow Somersets, linen from Flanders, silks from the east brought by Venetian merchants, wine from France, dried fruits from the Levant, a host of luxury goods, glass, jewels, furs, local wool from the Cotswolds, imported wool from Spain, lead from the Mendips, the works of goldsmiths, silversmiths, and iron-smiths, ribbons, trinkets, souvenirs innumerable, household goods, livestock and grain, surrounded and penetrated by a mob of players, dancers, quacks, preachers, beggars, and thieves, but this would be an exercise unwarranted by the information we have at our disposal, and would have the danger of making the event appear much more important and diverse than it probably was – Barton Fields was not Winchester, Stourbridge, or London, and it is probable that Bath fairs bore about the same sort of comparison with the great ones as a local agricultural show and gymkhana bears to the Bath and West.

Similarly, we have very limited knowledge of the appearance of medieval Bath for its buildings were destroyed by an idea, the eighteenth-century vision of Roman architecture, 'solid, proportionable, according to the rules, masculine and unaffected', and the only illustrations we have of the old town date from the end of our period. By this time Bath was largely a city of stone, a typical house being narrow, four storeys high, with a gable-end facing the street. Windows were divided by stone mullions, surmounted by dripstones, and the better houses had bays. A good example, though largely rebuilt since the war, is Hetling House (now Abbey Church House) which was put up as a town house for Sir Walter Hungerford in about 1570. Other gabled houses, although with sash windows and of the later seventeenth century, are in Broad Street and Green Street. The oldest house is Sally Lunn's house (no. 3 Lilliput Alley), built for the Duke of Kingston in 1480 but the front is seventeenth century. To what extent the early city conformed to the more customary style of half-timbering and thatched roof we do not know, but much of medieval Bristol, which also had good access to stone, was in this fashion, and there is no particular reason why Bath was not much the same.

Around the little city of some 1,500 souls (calculated from a Poll Tax return) was a battlemented stone wall with turrets, banked behind and descending to a ditch on the outside, which formed a convenient rubbish dump – in 1369 the mayor was ordered to see to 'the walls and turrets which are broken down in some places and liable to fall in others, and the dykes round the walls, which are obstructed by trees and grass growing in them and by dung and other filth thrown into them'. In the walls were the four main gates (see map, p. 44). Three of these, which were taken down in the eighteenth century, were substantial, about 10 feet (3 metres) wide, and the West Gate incorporated a large house used for lodging important visitors. The fourth, or East Gate, smaller and simpler, leading down to the river, can still be seen behind the Guildhall, well below the present ground level. In addition the Prior had the Lodyate (called St Peter's Gate) to the east of the Priory church, and the Ham Gate, near which issued an outflow from the Baths known as the Bum Ditch (later culverted). In the north-west corner the wall was rather higher, for according to Leland, 'One Gascoyne an Inhabitant of the Toune . . . made a little Peace of the Walle that was in Decay, as for a fine for a faught that he had committid in the Cite; whereof one part of a Corner risith higher than the Residew of the Walle, whereby it is commonly called Gascoyne-Tower.' Part of the 'Residew of the Walle' can be seen opposite the Mineral Water Hospital, although the top part is a Victorian reconstruction.

The medieval street pattern and its relationship to the present-day layout is shown on the map, p. 44 which demonstrates, as indeed the street names suggest, that most of the line of the walls can be walked today. Another feature the map shows are the four city churches which have disappeared. By the time of Wood's map of 1736 St Mary's Within (by the Northgate) had become King Edward's Grammar School and St Mary of Stalls had disappeared, its ruinous tower taken down in 1656. St Michael Within soon went, but St James's, by the South Gate, remained, with rebuildings and additions, until, after being bombed in 1941, it was demolished in 1955 to make way for Woolworth's. There may – or may not – be a moral in this.

Water conveyed from springs north and south of the city to 'conduits' in the streets was quite adequate for modest medieval wants, and by the sixteenth century 'many Houses yn the Toune have pipes of Leade to convey Water from Place to Place'. In fact, this little town with its water supply, its orchards and gardens, its surrounding fields, must have been a good deal more pleasant and healthy than the popular idea of the medieval town would suggest, although we must remember that the town ditch would be an offence to the nostrils, that the streets, in spite of scavenging pigs and dogs and the occasional removal of refuse would be little better, and the houses would be dark and crowded. It was, however, the in-filling of the seventeenth century which created the crowded conditions which Wood so severely criticised in the eighteenth, and this marks a change in the life and function of Bath which in no small measure dates from the death of the monastery at the Dissolution and the single government of the whole city under the charter of Elizabeth I.

5 *A* **B**od*y* **C**orporate
Tudor Bath

The Tudor period saw the end of the division of Bath
between Mayor and Prior, the disappearance of monastic
life, and the passing of much monastic land into private
hands. The Corporation grew in power and property, and
received a new Charter under which the City was to be
governed for nearly two and a half centuries until the
Municipal Corporations Reform Act of 1835. These
changes stemmed from the dissolution of the monastery.

In 1534, by the Act of Supremacy, Henry VIII took the
place of the Pope as Head of the Church of England, and
the following year his Vicar General, Thomas Cromwell,
sent out Commissioners to report on the revenues and righte-
ousness of the monasteries. To Bath came Dr Richard
Layton, a worldly prelate, who reported that the Priory had
annual revenues worth £617 2s 6d, second in Somerset after
Glastonbury, and 'the house well repaired but foure hundred
powndes in dett'. Prior Holeweye (otherwise Gibbs) was 'a
right vertuose man . . . simple and not of the greteste
witt' and not, apparently, a strong disciplinarian, for his
monks were reported as 'worse than I have any founde yet,
both in bugerie and adulterie'. Possibly – although the
Commissioners were hardly impartial! Layton, for example,
not being able to discover active misdemeanour at Glastonbury, resorted to the desperate expedient of reporting that

the monks would have *liked* to be naughty but the Abbot would not let them. It is not surprising that Gibbs (or Holeweye) tried to sweeten Cromwell with a pair of Irish falcons, a book of Anselm's works, and an annuity of £5. Incidentally, Layton sent a present himself: 'Ye shalle receive a bowke of our Ladies Miracles well able to match the Canterberrue Tailles. Such a bowke of dremes as ye never sawe which I fownde in the librarie.'

Bath, by reason of its revenues, escaped the Suppression in 1536 of the £200-a-year Lesser Monasteries, but soon Gibbs bowed to the inevitable and together with the Prior of Dunster, the daughter house, surrendered his property to the King on 27 January 1539. In return he received a pension of £9 a year and a house in Stall Street, while his 20 monks got pensions varying from £8 to £4 13s 4d. These were not ungenerous terms, although in those times of debased coinage and rising prices the older men would have found life difficult. The Prior had another source of sorrow if we are to believe Thomas Charnock's *Breviary of Natural Philosophy*, written in 1557. According to this the Prior was an alchemist, so successful in using the natural heat of Bath waters for his experiments that he had attained the final goal – 'He had our Stone, our Medicine, our Elixir, and all'. This he hid in a wall 'when the Abbie was supprest' and doubtless looked forward to a happy retirement of turning base metals into gold. What a terrible shock for the old man when he returned ten days later to find nothing left but the stopper!

> Then he told me he was in such Agonie,
> That for the loss thereof he thought he should be frenzie;
> And a toy (fancy) tooke him in the head to run such a race,
> That many a yeare after he had no settling place:
> And more, he is darke and cannot see,
> But hath a Boy to lead him through the country.

Poor crazed, blind, old Holeweye, alias Gibbs! We cannot

tell if the tale is true, but it seems to fit with the 'right vertuose man . . . not of the greteste witt' – He had lost his Priory, he had lost his Elixir – no wonder he also lost his reason.

It is impossible to assess the effect of the dissolution on the economic and social activity of the town; probably it was not great. There was, however, a considerable change in land-use and it is difficult today to imagine the long range of monastic buildings stretching south from the Abbey, the encircling walls and gates of the precincts, and the extensive Abbey orchard, for all this was sold off. The materials of the dormitory were bought by Robert Cocks, those of the fratry (refectory) by Sir Walter Denys, and the cloisters by Henry Bewchyn, while Ralph Hopton, ancestor of the Cavalier general, purchased other monastic buildings.

The church was offered to the city for 500 marks, but it was refused for the curious reason that the price was too low: 'the townsmen, fearing if they bought it so cheape to be thought to cozin the King, so that the purchase might come under the compasse of the concealed lands, refused the proffer'. It was then stripped of its lead, bells, glass and iron, and the shell was sold, with the Priory land in the City to Humphrey Coles for £962 17s 9d. Two days later he sold out to Matthew Coulthurst, MP for Bath, whose son Edmund in 1572 offered the carcass of the church to the City as a gift. This time they accepted, made Edmund a Freeman, and proceeded to use the gift as building material – 'Paide for carriadge of ij lode of stone from the Abbay to the guildhalle viij d'.

It was not until over 30 years after the Dissolution and 12 years after the gift, that some effort was made to render the church usable, when, in 1572 Peter Chapman paid for the repair of the east end of the north aisle. Two years later, after her visit, Elizabeth granted Letters Patent authorising collections throughout the kingdom for seven years for rebuilding the church, but according to Sir John Harington who lived in nearby Kelston not all the money got through:

11 The west front of the Abbey, from a print of 1750

12 The Abbey nave and choir

And thus the Church lies still, like the poore traveller mentioned in the 10th Luke, spoiled and wounded by thieves. The Priest goes by, the Levites go by, but doe nothing: only a good Samaritan, honest Mr Billet (worthy to be *billeted* in the New Jerusalem) hath powr'd some oyle in the wounds and maintained it in life.

Thomas Bellot (*Billet* only for the pun), steward to the great Lord Burleigh, was a man of high office, influence, and great charity, who 'faythfully distributed his Lord's and his owne wealth to the redifyinge of churches, founding of hospitals, sucoringe wonderfull number of poore' to such an extent, and notably at Bath, that he had little to leave – and of that 70 'poore honest' men of London parishes got 10s each. He died in 1611, and the following year Burleigh's son, Robert Cecil, Earl of Salisbury, with Bellot's nephew and namesake in his service, visited the church 'where old Master Bellot had bestowed some money of his father's . . . and a great part likewise of his own substance . . . And because ould Mr Bellot had spent all upon charitable uses and left nothinge for his kinsman, my lord in the churche saide "I give to my servant Bellot £20 a year during his naturall life".' It was probably the nephew who presented the 'great Communion Cupp of Silver with a Couer of Silver therto, both double guilt'.

The main work to the church was on the south transept, where the date 1576 can be seen carved on an outside buttress, the tower, to which a large clock was added and one of the bells from the old Keynsham Abbey installed, the great east window which today we see as a modern restoration, and the paving and furnishing of the east end of the church, including the Bellot font, of which the cover still remains. The nave, however, remained unroofed, and the completion of the work had to wait for the support of Bishop Montagu (1608–16) in the reign of James I. Sir John Harington claimed credit for this, with the aid of a violent rain storm from which he invited the Bishop to shelter in

the north aisle. The Bishop complained he was still getting
wet. 'How can that be,' asked Sir John, 'seeing we are
within the church?' 'True, but your church is unroofed, Sir
John.' 'The more the pity,' replied the knight, 'and the
more doth it call for the munificence of your lordship.'
Montagu, although he died Bishop of Winchester, now lies
in the dry on the north side of the nave where his recumbent
effigy may be seen. His bother, Sir Henry, 'beautified' the
oak west doors with the (restored) carving we see today.

The Jacobean ceiling to the nave was in wood and plaster,
similar to the one in the seventeenth-century vestry, and the
present fan-vaulting there dates from the restoration by Sir
George Gilbert Scott (of Albert Memorial and St Pancras
Station fame) in 1864–71, and none the worse for that.
Earlier restoration work was done in 1835 by C. P. Manners,
City Architect, in the first flood of the Gothic Revival when
the Victorian architect knew better than the medieval mason
what was Gothic and what was not. The ignorant Tudor
builder had failed to put flying buttresses along the nave;
Manners corrected this. The tower had no pinnacle! Advice
was sought of Mr Garbett of Winchester who said that
pinnacles would certainly have been *intended* and so, against
some local opposition, they were added. The square turrets
on the east end were made more romantically octagonal.
The parapet was 'enriched'. More practically, the clock was
removed to the north transept, the stone roofs were replaced
with lead and the clutter of funerary monuments was moved
to the sides where, as a Victorian Harington wrote,

> These walls adorned with monument and bust,
> Show how Bath waters serve to lay the dust.

At the same time the fine wrought-iron communion rail by
William Edney of Bristol, the gift of General Wade, was removed and sold to William Beckford for balconies. It was returned in 1959 and is now used as a grille. Finally, in 1859–
1901, the west front was restored by Sir T. G. Jackson
who in 1923 added the present cloisters as a war memorial.

And so we have the Abbey as it stands today, but no longer a Corporation church, for the 1835 Corporation Act abolished civic patronage and the advowson of the Abbey was acquired by the Simeon Trust, founded in 1836 by the Rev Charles Simeon, a Cambridge evangelical divine so that 'properly instructed' evangelical incumbents could be appointed. The Abbey continues to be the parish church of the central part of the city, a position it attained when Elizabeth granted the advowsons of the other city churches to the Corporation. Citizen control brought about the disappearance of two churches, St Mary of Stalls, and St Mary's Within, and the leasing of land close to the Abbey after 1584 for house-building with the result that houses huddled against the church constricting the passage from the Abbey churchyard to such an extent, until General Wade made his Passage, that folk commonly used the north aisle as the easiest way through. The houses were not demolished until the 1830s and the mark of a gable can still be seen on the wall of the north aisle.

The rest of the Abbey grounds, including the Orchard, also passed via Coles to Coulthurst who in 1584 was occupying the Priory House. In 1611 they were sold to John Hall, a wealthy clothier of Bradford-on-Avon, progenitor of a line which subsequently acquired the titles of Duke of Kingston, Baron Pierrepont, Viscount Newark, and Earl Manvers, all commemorated by street names in Bath. However Edward vi by Letters Patent of 12 July 1552 had granted Priory land to the Corporation for the endowment of a Grammar School and an almshouse, and this gave rise to a lawsuit in 1620 between the city and the sitting tenant, John Biggs. Biggs maintained that the land belonged to John Hall, that the Orchard, through which the Corporation claimed right of way, had always been reckoned part of the Priory House, and that it was privileged property, for when the Mayor came into it 'the Maces were put down and not carried before them'. For good measure he objected to the Corporation witnesses who were, he claimed, Almsmen

dependent upon Corporation charity, and therefore prejudiced.

Edward's grant had already caused trouble for he had
preceded it in 1550 with Letters Patent granting that
Humphrey Cotton, a Bath physician, should have for life
the office of Keeper of the Baths with a fee of 4d a day
providing one bath was to be free for the poor. Cotton
complained in a letter to the Queen that, although he had
for three years 'continued and exercised the same, susteyning
great costs labour and travill in and aboute at adaptyng
purgyng clenyng and repayring of the same', the Mayor,
Edward Ludwell, and the ex-Mayor, Richard Chapman
(both MPS) were constantly interfering with him, had 'pro-
cured and maynteyned dyverse other lewd persons to do the
like unto hym', and, 'still percerveryng in their devilishe
mynde', had taken the keys of the 'Baynes' 'to the utter
undoyng forever of your pore Subject his wyf and nyne pore
children'. He wanted his keys back and to be allowed 'quiet
possession and occupacion of the premysses'. The case went
to arbitration, and Cotton was ordered to hand over the
property, in recompense for which the Corporation was to
pay him 'fowerscore and ten poundes of lawfull money of
Englonde'.

The Corporation farmed out the job of Keeper of the
Baths. In 1581, for instance, Anthony Lovell paid 20s for
Keeping the Hot Bath, and from 1583 to 1596 as Keeper
of the King's Bath paid 40s a year, while in 1588 and 1590
John Stangwadge paid 2s for the Lower Baths. Their income
came mainly from tips. The Corporation also appointed
lesser officials with the grand title of *Directores Balnei* whose
work was to provide linen, attend the bathers, and pump
water over them when required. One of the Keeper's jobs
was to see to the cleansing of the Baths. In Leland's time
they were 'commonly shut up from halfe an houre after ten
of the clocke in the forenoone, to halfe an houre after one
in the afternoone, and likewaise at midnight: at which time
the keeper of them resorteth to his charge, opening the

gates, and leaveth (or should leave) free passage unto such as come to them.' It was hopefully believed that while the baths were closed 'they purge themselves furthermore from all such filth as the diseased doo leave in each of them'. By 1634 the baths were emptied and cleansed weekly, except for the Cross Bath, which being smaller and more frequently used was cleansed twice a week.

The baths acquired by the Corporation were the King's, the Cross, and the Hot – the Prior's, which was fed from the King's, having fallen into disuse. These can still be seen in their rebuilt eighteenth- and nineteenth-century forms; indeed the Cross and the Hot (now called the Old Royal) are still in use. What they were like about 1540 we can find from Leland's account.

The King's Bath was the largest, 'very faire and large . . . compassid with a high Stone Waulle'. Round the 'Brimmes' was a low stone wall with 32 arches for men and women to stand in separately. The overflow ran a mill and then joined the Avon above Bath Bridge through what in Speed's map is called the Bum Ditch. Speed also shows a covered gallery running round the Bath, private cabins ('slips') at the corners, a decorative spire in the middle and a drinking fountain.

A fountain is mentioned in 1599 when the Chamberlain 'paid for stones and carryage to make [either construct or repair] the fountayne in the King's Bath and for lyme and to the masons, Gardner and Biddell, and those that did help him about the same work xxxvij s', and is described by Dr Pierce in 1697 as a pyramidical hollow stone with a copper spout from which people received the waters 'sincere from the spring'. Drinking the water, said Pierce, was an ancient custom and served 'to quench Thirst and to keep Soluble' . . .

for it had been long observed and now very well known that a draught or two of the Bath Water quencheth thirst better than double the quantity of Beer or Ale, or any other usual Beverage; and when by spending the moistures in long and much sweating, the Bowels were heated, and dry'd and rendred Constipate; a large draught of this Water with a little common Salt, would infallibly give a Stool or two.

It is apparent (Sarah Gamp would say 'aperient') that heated Bowels in Bristol, Gloucester, Worcester, and London could benefit, for Henry Chapman recorded in 1673 that the waters were bottled and sent to these towns. He also mentioned the sluices at the King's Bath as maintaining the water level 'so that Dame Luna, that Piddling Piss-kitchen-plant, with her Ebbings and Flowings, her Nepes and Spring-tides, hath no Interference at all here'. Today, visitors can drink the waters in the Pump Room or from an outside fountain, but their motive is more curiosity than anything else.

From the Pump Room can be seen the remains of the King's Bath. Its water is as Leland described it, apart from the colour, which is yellowish. 'The colour of the water of the Baynes', he wrote, 'is as it were a depe blew Se Water, and rikith like a sething Potte continually, having a sulpherous and sumwhat an onpleasant savour.' On its walls may be seen rings donated by grateful bathers, a tablet commemorating Bladud, mythical founder of Bath, and a portion of a stone balustrade. Another tablet on the south wall reads: 'Sir Francis Stonor of Stonor in the County of Oxon Kt trubled with gout and aches in the limbs received benefit by ye bath and living many years after well in health and to the age of 90 in memory of the same gave the stone rails about ye bath in the year 1697.' This date appears to be wrong. Guidott and Wood both give it as 1624, a year when Sir Francis was in Bath, and his balustrade was repaired in 1630. The Bladud inscription, which was probably originally fixed to the door of the bath, reads with unwarrantable assurance:

Bladud Son of Lud Hudibras eighth king of the Britains from Brute a great philosopher and mathematician bred

at athens and recorded the first discoverer and founder of
these baths eight hundred sixty three years before christ
that is two thousand five hundred sixty two years to the
present year 1699.

What one cannot see is the adjoining Queen's Bath for
it was demolished in Victorian times when the underlying
Roman Circular Bath was disinterred. Its establishment is
part of the long history of Disputes of Bath, for it came
from a Star Chamber award relating to a dispute between
the Corporation and the citizens about a way stopped up
between Stall Street and the King's Bath. In the award it is
recorded that the Mayor and Corporation had promised to
build a women's bath adjacent to the King's Bath and get it
done before Whitsun 1576. Men might use it 'in the
absence of women'. At first called the New Bath, it became
the Queen's in 1613 when it was visited by Anne of
Denmark, consort of James I.

Wood's *Essay* of 1749 contains the unsubstantiated story
that the Queen was frightened from the King's Bath by 'a
Flame of Fire, like a Candle, which had no sooner ascended
to the top of the Water than it spread itself into a large
Circle of Light, and then became extinct' and so removed
herself to the New Bath whose building he attributes, again
without evidence, to Bellot. Wood is on firmer ground in
saying that the citizens erected a Tower or Cross in the
middle of the Bath in the Queen's honour, finished at the
top with a Crown over a Globe on which was written in letters
of gold ANNA REGINA SACRUM. Later this was taken down
and the globe fashioned into a drinking font for the new
Pump Room of 1790. A similar inscription, ANNA REGINA
SACRUM 1618, appears as a pierced parapet to a large house
overlooking the bath in Johnson's drawing of 1675.

The King's outflow supplied not only the Queen's Bath
but also the Horse Bath shown in Speed's map with an
appropriate horse lying in it. This was just outside the town
walls, to the west of Southgate Street which in the eighteenth

century was called Horse Street. The other two baths had their own 'sprynges of whote Water'. The Cross Bath, so called because of the 'Cross erectid in the middle' was the larger and had 12 alcoves for 'men to stonde under in tyme of Rayne'. It was 'temperate', and 'much frequentid of People diseased with Lepre, Pokkes, Scabbes, and great Acnes'. The other had only seven alcoves and was called the Hot Bath because 'at cumming into it, Men think it wold scald the Flesch at the first, but after that the Flesch ys warmid it is more tolerable and pleasant'.

After Leland's time, it appears, some alterations were made, for example a new, smaller, cross was put in the Cross Bath, the Hot Bath was enlarged, and an arcaded wall put round it and pumps installed for sluicing the bathers. A new, 12-foot square, Lazours' (Lepers') Bath was added to the Hot Bath and is first mentioned in 1598 when the Chamberlain paid for nails for it. Apparently it was converted into an underground tank when the younger Wood rebuilt the Hot Bath in 1777. For the housing of the lepers a small hospital was build by John de Feckenham, last Abbot of Westminster, in 1576. It was demolished in 1804.

The improvements may well have been done for the visit of Queen Elizabeth in the hot August of 1574, for this not surprisingly galvanised the Corporation into a flurry of make-do-and-mend, as the Chamberlain's accounts show.

The city walls with their rubbish dumps were cleaned up, a painter from Salisbury was paid four guineas and fourpence for smartening up Northgate, Westgate, and the King's Bath, while one, Chedgey, received 6s for 'dressing' Southgate. St Catharine's Hospital, popularly known as the Black Alms, was floored, which must have been a comfort to the 'fourteen poor women' within. This was the 'new almshouse', the object, with the Grammar School, of King Edward's confusing charity. It can still be seen in its restored form. Stones were hauled from the Abbey to repair the Guildhall, which then stood in the middle of the High Street, and the Abbey itself was decorated in greenery in an attempt to mitigate its sorry appearance. The windows in Stall's church were repaired and 'quiresters' imported from Wells; the City Bellman was given a new coat of 'black frise at xv pence the yard'; and the City gelding was 'dressed' for its lameness. For the inevitable requirements the city took care to put up a new privy – with crest. An interesting improvement was the paving 70 yards 'by goodwiffe Bedfordes dore', a special attention which suggests that the goodwiffe might have caused some embarrassment if it had not been done. It hardly seems to have been enough for when there was a projected second visit in 1602, which did not materialise, the Corporation hastily sent 'unto Tetburie and unto Cicister to get paviers against the Queene's coming'.

In 1590, 16 years after her visit, the Queen granted the city a new Charter which was of considerable importance for it set the Corporation firmly in control of a considerably enlarged town. This charter defined the rights, privileges, and duties of the Municipality, based on those already established, it defined the bounds, and it nominated the officers, William Sherston, who owned a good deal of the newly-included land, being named Mayor. From then onwards all vacancies were to be filled by vote of the Mayor, recorder, aldermen, and other councillors.

The Corporation was to be a Body able and capable to purchase and grant lands, to plea and be impleaded, and to have a seal which they could 'make, break, or re-make'. It was also empowered to make laws and set penalties provided they were not 'repugnant nor contrary to the laws and statutes of our realm of England'. Judicial business was carried out by the Mayor, two aldermen annually elected as Justices of the Peace, a Common Clerk, who was to be 'an honest and discreet man', and a Recorder who had to combine the same qualities with being 'learned in the laws of the land'. The first Recorder was an *Esquire*, while the first Clerk was only a *Gent*.

To enforce the law there were two bailiffs who had control of the gaol, which shared the tower of St Mary's with the

Grammar School. There was also a pillory in High Street, two pairs of stocks (one by the pillory, the other by the Hot Bath), a ducking-stool on Boat-stall Quay, a rack, and a cage. When not engaged in filling these, the bailiffs managed the markets. Inferior officers included constables, boundary-supervisors, meat inspectors, leather searchers, ale-tasters, a bellman, and a beadle. The penalty for refusing office was gaol and a 'reasonable' fine.

Cases were heard in a Court Leet, twice a year. The Court could not deal with major offences such as murder, rape, arson, and burglary, but it had a wide range of powers over lesser offences, mostly connected with property and trade. These included encroachments, interference with buildings or fences, waters stopped or deviated, receiving stolen goods, clipping and forging coins, treasure trove, and the selling of under-weight or sub-standard goods, principally bread and ale.

Income came mainly from rents, including the rent of the Common, at that time leased by Mr Peter Beshyn (Bewshine, Bowshine, or Bowshin – imaginative spelling, even for the sixteenth century). At the Dissolution the Prior had naturally lost his rights in the Common Lands and this led to a certain amount of confusion. Litigation with the freeholders in 1619 resulted in an award by Nicholas Hyde, Recorder of Bath, whereby the citizens received in lieu of right of common an area of freehold known as High, Middle, and Low Common. These have been important in the history of the town's physical development as they effectively cut short the spread of Georgian Bath to the west and this alienation of valuable building land created further disputes in the nineteenth century. The land today comprises parks, allotments, and a golf course.

The baths brought in little money, but it is surprising that the Chamberlain's accounts show no income from the market, established by a Charter of Henry VIII, although expenditure on it is recorded.

Outgoings were largely on the upkeep of property, on

water supply and sanitation, on highways, on the baths and market, and on supporting the poor. Money was also spent on entertainments and gifts to distinguished visitors. The Lord Admiral's, Lord Chamberlain's, and Queen's players visited the city several times, so it is not impossible that Shakespeare himself came to Bath.

Not a great deal was spent on sanitation, which in a city of many gardens and open spaces was not perhaps too serious a matter, although Sir John Harington thought otherwise. Linking Godliness with Cleanliness, he wrote in 1591:

> The fair church her Highness gave orders should be re-edified stands at a stay; and the common sewer which before stood in an ill place, stands now in no place, for they have not any at all; which for a town so plentifully served with water, in a country so well provided with stone, in a place resorted to so greatly, methinks seems an unworthy and dishonourable thing.

Sir John's interest in hygiene is not surprising, as he had invented the first water closet. 'A man I met at Raleigh's,' wrote a contemporary, 'John Harington, Bess's godson, had invented a privy that could be drained with water. You pulled a little handle and water gushed from a cistern above. He had scented water for the ladies. But people won't be clean. They think he's mad or merely dirty-minded.'

One more concern of the Corporation is worth mentioning. In the embattled England of Elizabeth, ever conscious of the Spanish threat, the government of even such a little, inland, 'somewhat decayed', town had to have a care for national defence. Bath, with its seven archers, eight pikemen, and four 'gonners' recorded in the Muster Roll of 1569, along with its four corselets, two pairs of 'almain rivets', two calibers, and one harquebus, had hardly a massive contribution to make, but the Corporation took some care to maintain its scanty equipment. Accounts show 4d for 'stuffing a headpiece' and 2d for 'stuffing a murion', while in 1598 the city spent 6d on 'playstering of a little chamber where the armour lyeth', 'bought nine bullett baggs and mended three more, bought a capp for a headpiece, mended a muskett, bought cloth for three soldiers coats, with six dozen and a half of lace', and in the next year 'paid William Doulton for repayring of faults in the citties armour'.

The little band of citizens was never called upon to fight, but the city may have some small claim to fame in the defence arrangements, for in 1586, according to the Privy Council records, it nearly mobilised the nation. 'A casual fier happening about the cittie of Bath, the country was like to have risen, the watchers of the Beacons neere thereabout supposing the same to have been a Becon fired.'

It is difficult, with limited evidence, to assess the effect on the town of the Tudor changes. The Corporation was a closed, powerful, self-perpetuating body, responsible to no one but itself, and with the sole right to nominate and elect the city's representatives in Parliament. Austin J. King, writing in 1888, in the full tide of Victorian city pride, had no doubt at all. 'The vices inherent in the system of government', he firmly wrote, 'were horrible.' It would have been possible, of course, for the Corporation to have concerned itself entirely with lining its own pockets, but there is no evidence that its conduct was at all scandalous, and the charge that can be most effectively levelled is not that it was evil, but that it was inert. As we shall see, the revival of Bath was to owe more to private enterprise than to official zeal.

6 Garrison Town
The Seventeenth Century

Economically, the growth of Bath was to depend on an influx of wealthy visitors. The sick poor had always been there, and it was for them that Abbot Feckenham of Westminster built the little Elizabethan hospital for lepers near the Cross Bath. This has disappeared but we can still see Bellot's almshouse in its reconstructed form of 1869. This may have amplified Freckenham's foundation. Impoverished visitors constituted an increasing problem under the Elizabethan Poor Law Act of 1601 which made the relief of the poor a parish responsibility, and special arrangements were made in the Act which were later to become a general system for the country. 'Whereas', it was promulgated, 'a great number of poor and diseased people do resort to the City of Bath in the County of Somerset, and the Town of Buxton in the County of Derby, for some ease and relief of their diseases at the baths there, and by means thereof the inhabitants of the same city of Bath and town of Buxton are greatly overcharged with the same poor people, to their intolerable charge', such people would not be allowed to visit without a licence in which the home parish agrees to be responsible for them if they become paupers, 'and that the inhabitants of the same city and town shall not in any wise be charged by this Act with the finding of relief of any such poor people'. With no certificate and no money you would come under the Act for the Punishment of Rogues and Vagabonds, with unpleasant consequences – if you were caught (it was said that in 1596 in Somerset a fifth part of felonies were not brought to trial).

It was not therefore of the poor that the Mayor was thinking when he wrote that 'it hath been the ill hap of our Country Bathes to lye more obscure than any other throughout Christendom', nor was it the illiterate masses he was considering when he put down the obscurity to a lack of publicity, saying that it was 'because very few have written about it'. Whether he had rightly diagnosed the trouble or not it is a fact that the increased popularity of Bath with the wealthier classes coincided with a spate of medical books, starting with one by William Turner MD, chaplain and physician to the Lord Protector Somerset, and then consecutively made Dean of Wells, exiled under Mary and reinstated under Elizabeth only to be suspended for nonconformity. In his Preface he expressly stated that his purpose in writing about Bath was 'to allure thyther as manye as have nede of such helpe as almighty God hath graunted it to give'.

Another treatise, *The Bathes of Bathes Ayde*, was published in 1572, the work of John Jones, a physician of Bath, in which Dr Guidott, a century later, found 'things not contemptible . . . yet nothing of the true Nature is there discovered, only, as in all former Writers of Baths, chiefly Catholick, a strong Stench of Sulphur, and a great ado about a Subterranean Fire, a fit resemblance to Hell, at least of Purgatory'. In 1620 came Tobias Venner's *Via Recta ad Vitam Longam . . . with the true use of the Baths at Bath*, followed in 1631 by the influential *Discourse of Naturell Bathes and Mineral Waters . . . especially of our Bathes at Bathe* by Edward Jordan, scholar of Oxford and Padua, who settled in Bath and had a great reputation as a physician. Twelve years later there appeared a work in Latin *Thermae Bathonicae* by Thomas Johnson, and then in 1676 Dr Guidott's own book *A Discourse of Bath and the hot waters there*.

While the physicians saw to the publicity the citizens set about improving the accommodation. 'The City of Bath,' says a contemporary account, 'being both poor enough and proud enough since her Highness [Elizabeth] being here, wonderfully beautified itself in fine houses for victualling and lodging', so that soon it could be written that 'Bath . . . is a little well-compacted Cittie, and beautified with very faire and goodly buildings for receit of strangers', and 'The buildings of the city are sufficiently numerous, large, and commodious, for the reception of the stream of sick persons from all parts who, seeking the cure of their disease, flock hither annually in Spring and Autumn as to the sacred Temple of Hygeia.' It seems likely therefore that there was a great deal of new building and of refacing of old structures in the seventeenth century. Accommodating visitors became a major occupation of leading citizens.

The reputation of the place was enhanced by Royal visits and it is to be hoped that this repaid the cost of their entertainment. The first visit was in 1613 by Anne of Denmark, Queen to James I, when the Corporation seemed to have found a little difficulty in raising the money for her presentation cup. Incidentally her faith in the natural waters was not extended to the local brewing, for she brought her own beer supply. On her second visit, in 1615, her 'waymen, littermen, footmen, coachmen, trumpeters, porters, guards, and drummers' all received gifts from the City and, 'Peter the blind man' received 5s for 'playing on the Organs at the Queen's lying here'. A pretty woman, but frivolous, expensive, stupid, and suffering from dropsy, she claimed that the waters did her good, which might explain her son's visit when he was King.

Charles I came in July 1628 and his Queen, Henrietta Maria, in 1634. She, however, was dissatisfied with the cure and transferred to Bourbon, where the circumstances and entertainment were more to her French tastes. It was about this time that she, albeit indirectly, caused a Bath man to lose his ears. The man was William Prynne (1600–64), grandson of William Sherston, born at Swainswick, and educated at King Edward's Grammar School and Oriel College, Oxford. He was an effective and industrious Puritan pamphleteer and in 1663 published *Historio-mastix*, a violent attack on stage plays and on the kings, emperors, empresses, and actresses who performed. Unfortunately for him Henrietta Maria had taken part in a masque and the pamphlet was taken as a direct insult. After a year in the Tower he was sentenced by the Star Chamber to be fined £5,000, expelled from Lincoln's Inn, degraded of his degree, pilloried, deprived of his ears, and imprisoned for life – a rather savage piece of literary criticism. All this was carried out except the fine and part of the imprisonment. The tale of the controversies of this man of deep conscience, bitter pen, and contentious disposition, is too long to tell here except to note that he lost the stumps of his ears for assailing the bishops and was branded SL (seditious libeller) which he maintained stood for *stigmata Laudis* (the mark of archbishop Laud), was in and out of prison, opposed the Regicides, and was MP for Bath from 1660 onwards. He died, unmarried, in his lodgings at Lincoln's Inn on 24 October 1664.

As a social centre Bath was not very exciting. Tennis and bowls, bag-pipe players and waits, bear-baiting and acrobats, and the occasional visit of a company of players, add up to rather meagre entertainment, but they are all we have evidence for. A tennis court is shown on Speed's map (1610) to the east of the King's Bath, and 'one wooden barton called Tennysepley' close to St James's was leased to Alderman Thomas Gibbs on 24 June 1585. A manuscript of about this time said that close to the Abbey are '2 curious Bowling Grounds, one of them is curiously and neatly kept, where onely Lords, Knights, Gallants, and Gentlemen, of the best ranke and qualitie, doe dayly meet in reasonable times to recreate themselves, both for pleasure and health'. The Old Bowling Green is shown to the south-east of the Abbey on Gilmore's map (1694) which also has a Fives

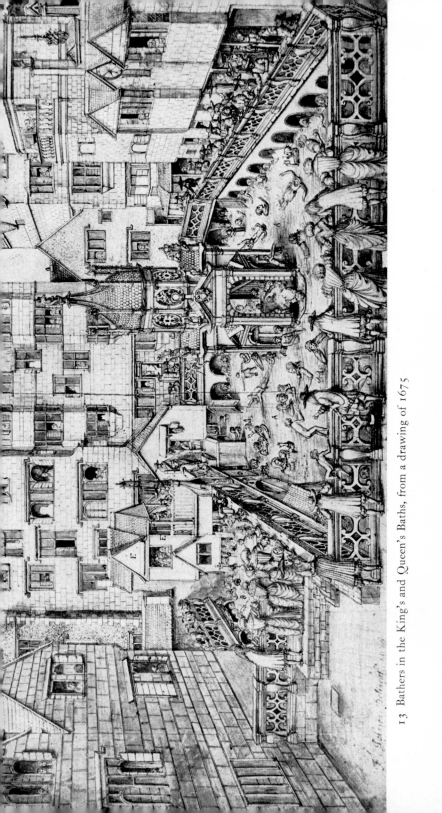

13 Bathers in the King's and Queen's Baths, from a drawing of 1675

14 Bath in 1610, from a map by John Speed

Court outside the West Gate and a Cockpit in Timber Green (now called Sawclose). The boom in even this limited entertainment was to come to an abrupt end, and the gentlemen of best rank and quality were to find sterner employment than playing bowls.

An account of 1642 satirised the state of collapse:

> Guides were necessitated to guide one another from the alehouse lest they should lose their practice; the ladies were fallen into a lethargy for want of stirring cavaliers to keep them awake, and the poor fiddlers were ready to hang themselves in their strings for want of other employment.

In January of that year the King left London and the sad story of strife with Parliament had reached an open break. Both sides endeavoured to raise troops, Parliament by a Militia Ordinance and Charles by a Commission of Array which Parliament immediately declared illegal. In August the Summer Assizes were being held in Bath and the Judge, Sir Robert Foster, was called upon by the Constable of Keynsham on behalf of some 20 Hundreds in Somerset and about the same in Devon, to read aloud in court Parliament's condemnation of the Commission of Array. He also received a strong letter from the Marquis of Hertford, who was on his way down from York, warning him that the gentlemen of Dorset were 'well affected to the King' and that they relied on his 'courage and constancy'. The Judge contented himself with a statement that it was unfortunate that people were confused by contradictory instructions and that both orders should be withdrawn.

When Hertford arrived he and the Judge were entertained by the Corporation with sack, claret, chickens, turkeys, and capons, but the Marquis soon left for Wells where, with Sir Ralph Hopton, he gathered forces for the King and moved westward to Wales while Hopton moved to Cornwall. With the departure of the Royalists the Parliamentarians moved in and the City, with professional hospitality, regaled their leaders with sack and claret, and cleaned up Lady Waller's tomb. (1643: 'Pd. the Sexton for keeping cleane Sir William Wallers Ladies Tombe of the last two yeares £2.') Sir William Waller, appointed by Parliament as Major-General in Gloucestershire, had seen service in Germany and was a soldier of considerable energy and daring whose early successes in the Civil War earned him the nickname 'William the Conqueror'. He may be seen on his tomb in the Abbey gazing thoughtfully at his wife, but she is the *first* Lady Waller, Jane, who died in 1633, and he himself is buried in London.

Bath was immediately put into a posture of defence. The walls were repaired and strengthened, especially by St James's; private doors in the wall were filled in; a platform was made at Gascoyne's Tower; drawbridges were installed, and the gates repaired; 'great guns' were hauled in over the bridge and installed; guard rooms ('Courts of Guard') were established, and the Guildhall was turned into an arsenal. Stocking the Guildhall with munitions had in fact an earlier history, and in order to make room for the Assizes the Corporation had to remove barrels of match, the fuse used for igniting the powder in muskets. Yet in this busy time (there were at least 12 'proclamacions' in the year) the Corporation found time to mend Goody Pitcher's 'chimbley' in Bimbery Lane, and to buy 26 yards of 'blew broad cloth' for the old people in St John's Hospital.

For a time it must have seemed to some of the citizens that they had taken a lot of trouble for nothing. The tide of war had moved away, the towns of Somerset were declaring for Parliament, and Rupert's attack on Bristol had been unsuccessful. The breathing-space was to be short. Down in Devon, in May 1643, the Earl of Stamford, to whom Bath had given 'a present' costing £1 8s 6d, was defeated by Hopton, and on 4 June Hopton, Prince Maurice, and Hertford joined together at Chard on the south Somerset border, with some 2,000 horse, 4,000 foot, including five Cornish regiments, 3,000 dragoons and 16 field guns.

Moving northwards the Royalist forces arrived on 10 June at Chewton Mendip, some dozen miles from Bath, where they were victorious in a cavalry skirmish with Waller's men. Hopton then wrote to his old friend and present opponent asking if they might meet, and Waller's reply epitomised the tragedy of sincere men caught up for conscience sake in unloved strife.

> Certainly my affections to you are so unchangeable, that hostility itself cannot violate my friendship to your person. But I must be true to the cause wherein I serve. . . . We are both upon the stage, and must act such parts as are assigned to us in this tragedy. Let us do it in a way of honour and without personal animosities, whatsoever the issue may be. . . .

Waller, with the main body of his troops, reinforced by Sir Arthur Hazelrigg's 'Lobsters', was at Bath, and it was in the hilly, broken country around the city that he intended to halt the Royalist advance. Hopton avoided the direct approach from the south, crossed the river at Bradford-on-Avon and moved northward towards Batheaston, with the intention of holding the Bath road to London. The way from Bradford ran first through the open plateau top and then along the steep-sided, wooded valley of the Avon. Here Waller set an ambush, bringing men over a bridge he built at Claverton, but the ambush was broken and the Parliamentarians were pursued through Bathampton to the southeast slopes of Lansdown, while Maurice's men took the Claverton bridge and stormed up the hill above toward Bathampton Down. But now, at midnight, all was darkness, confusion, and fatigue, so the Royalist army fell back on Bathampton where in the morning, gathering for attack, they saw Waller's forces commanding them from Lansdown: The opportunity for a successful attack on Bath from the east had gone, so Hopton withdrew his forces northwards to Marshfield that they might make the attempt from the north. In the grey light of the early morning of 5 July 1643,

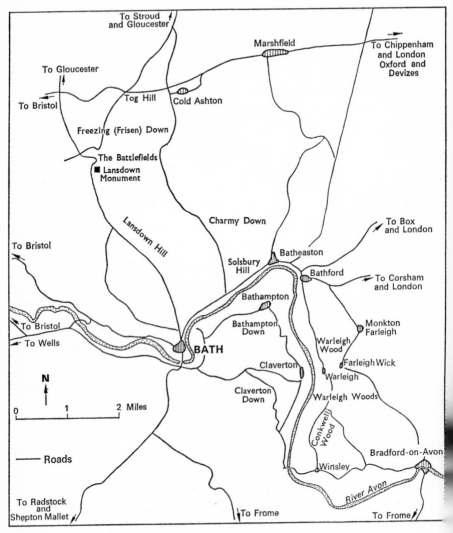

To Stroud and Gloucester

To Gloucester

To Bristol

Tog Hill

Cold Ashton

Marshfield

To Chippenham and London Oxford and Devizes

Freezing (Frisen) Down

The Battlefields

■ Lansdown Monument

Charmy Down

To Box and London

Lansdown Hill

Solsbury Hill

Batheaston

Bathford

To Corsham and London

To Bristol

Bathampton

Bathampton Down

Monkton Farleigh

To Bristol

To Wells

BATH

Claverton

Warleigh Wood

Farleigh Wick

Warleigh

N

Claverton Down

Warleigh Woods

0   1   2 Miles

Conkwell Wood

Bradford-on-Avon

—— Roads

Winsley

River Avon

To Radstock and Shepton Mallet

To Frome

To Frome

THE BATH AREA AT THE TIME OF THE BATTLE OF LANSDOWN 1643

the King's men moved westward to gather on Freezing Hill. At their feet lay a deep valley of muddy fields and twisting lanes while beyond steep wooded slopes led up to the broad smooth top of Lansdown, the way to Bath. And holding the brow of that hill were Waller's men.

During the night Waller, 'the best chooser and shifter of ground' that Colonel Slingsby knew, had anticipated the Royalist action and moved his troops from the south end to the northern tip of Lansdown, put up earthworks, mounted his cannon to command the valley, and filled the wood with musketeers. 'Thus fortified,' wrote Clarendon in his *History of the Great Rebellion*, 'stood the fox, gazing at us.'

Confident in the strength of his position, Waller sent in his cavalry who were at first so successful that in the afternoon Hopton decided to retire to join the King at Oxford, but the Royalists rallied, the infantrymen held, the tide of battle turned until the foot of Lansdown was in Royalist hands. But only the foot. Rearing above were slopes 'like the eaves of a house' and at the peak the menacing mouths of field artillery. It was then that the Cornish infantrymen cried that they would 'fetch down those cannon'. Three times they attempted the impossible, struggling upwards under a hail of shot and the shock of cavalry charges, blinded by smoke, hampered in the woodland by their 15-foot pikes, but inspired by supreme courage, indomitable stubbornness, and the leadership of their beloved Bevil Grenville. The third time they breasted the ridge – and stood, 'immovable as a rock'. Their position was perilous. 'One lusty charge', wrote Slingsby, 'would have rolled them down', but the Parliamentary cavalry was exhausted and, facing not only the pikemen but the musketeers, they could not break the line. As darkness fell Waller withdrew his men some 400 yards to the shelter of the stone walls which divided the fields.

The Royalists were in no condition to press home the attack and had suffered a psychological shock in the loss of Grenville, who was mortally wounded in the great assault. Through the night they watched the flickering fires in the enemy camp and it was only in the early hours of the next morning that they found that Waller had retired to Bath and the lights came from lengths of match left hanging on the walls. After the heroic efforts of the day before it was all rather an anti-climax and morale was lowered further when the explosion of an ammunition waggon, caused apparently by a prisoner's injudicious smoking, severely wounded Hopton, almost blinding him. Tired and shaken the army moved away, to be pursued by Waller, reinforced from Bristol, into Devizes. Here Hopton, ill as he was, held the town, while Maurice and Hertford broke through the enemy to fetch cavalry help from Oxford. Three days later Maurice returned with about 1,800 horse and in the extraordinary battle of Roundway Down, which the Royalists were to call 'Runaway Hill', they inflicted a crushing defeat on an enemy twice their number. A fortnight later Prince Rupert took Bristol and the Cornishmen took Bath, which for the next two years was held for the King, under the Governorship of Sir Thomas Bridges, at £7 a week, with a garrison of 140 men.

Today the battlefield lies silent and alone, with only a few dubious low lines of earthwork and near the road a monument erected in 1720 by Lord Lansdown, Grenville's grandson, to commemorate his illustrious ancestor. This monument bears an indifferent piece of verse. It was written in 1643 and does more to commemorate Richard 'thy valiant ancestor' than Bevil. More in keeping are the words of Clarendon engraved on another face – '. . . a brighter Courage and a Greater Disposition were never marryed together to make a more cheerful and innocent Conversation'.

The change of masters made little difference to the life of the town. Money still had to be found for ammunition, for 'candles and fires' for the Courts of Guards, and for 'presents' to the Governor, including a house. Rates were levied for the Royal cause – £150 for 'arreres to the King' and £40 for 'prence' Maurice. Work continued on the fortifications, but the blocking of the West Gate had proved such a nuisance that it was fitted with a drawbridge at the city's expense, the Governor supplying the wood. Straw was provided 'for sick soldiers' and 'milk for Prince Rupert's soldiers, being maimed'. The only mention of the Baths is 3s for a shroud and burial for a stranger drowned in the King's Bath, and the only records of any special hospitality are 'candells for the Queen' when Henrietta Maria came through in May 1644 on her way to Exeter where her daughter was shortly to be born, and £15 for a plate when the King himself was present in July. There is no mention of the visit of the Prince of Wales, the future Charles the Second, when he temporarily moved his court from Bristol to escape the plague. Indeed, the only mention of any sort of excitement was the ordering of wood for bonfires on 'crowne nation day'.

Two years after the Royalist victory at Roundway Down the King's forces were smashed at Naseby and the New Model Army under Fairfax, with Cromwell as his Lieutenant General of Horse, swept into the West, utterly defeated Goring at Langport ('To see this', said Cromwell, 'is it not to see the face of God?'), took Bridgwater, and quartered at Wells. On 29 July 1645, a brigade sent by Fairfax from Wells arrived at Bath, and Colonel Rich, in command of the cavalry, called upon the City to surrender. The demand was refused, but morale was not high. As night began to fall the defenders of the south gate were astonished to find that their muskets had acquired a will of their own, while voices outside demanded surrender. A party of dragoons had crawled across the bridge and seized the barrels of the weapons as they protruded through the loopholes. In amazement and confusion the defenders abandoned the gate which the attackers promptly fired. It was enough. Although the defences were still strong and the garrison well equipped a parley was called for, and the city surrendered. As was the practice, the 'common soldiers', about 140 of them, were taken prisoners, and the officers were allowed to march away. If they had held on the issue might have been different for Rupert was on his way from Bristol with 1,500 horse and foot, but on hearing of the surrender he turned back. The next day Fairfax himself visited, was regaled with wine and sugar, and left two regiments of foot as garrison before he moved on to Sherborne.

If life had been hard in the city before it was to get much worse as demands for money, horses, provisions and quartering poured in. There were disputes about the money to be found for the army, there were rates to be raised to support troops quartered on the town ('at 2s 6d for each man and horse'), the churches were filled with soldiers, their accoutrements and bedding, and on one occasion troops from Marlborough on their march westward requisitioned all the meal in the town, although afterwards they did 'restore it again to many of the poorer sort'. On the whole the troops did not behave badly but the strain they put on the city was almost insupportable and Bath constantly petitioned to have the garrison removed. The Mayor, writing to Captain Harington, put the matter succinctly. 'Our houses are emptied of all useful furniture, and much broken and disfigured; our poor suffer for want of victuals, and rich we have none. . . . I dare not send a man on horseback, as the horse would be taken.' No wonder that they tried to get recompense for the £100 they had lent to the Royalist Governor!

Affairs did not improve during the Commonwealth and on 9 June 1651 the Council decided to give no more money to 'the lame soldiers now in town, sent by order of Parliament' nor to any in future until they spare it from 'more urgent occasions'. 'Our City', they wrote, 'is much impoverished', and they were suitably grateful when in November 1652 Lord Skudamore made them a gift of £200, the five per cent interest to pay the stipend of 'a physician for poor visitors' (although we may wonder exactly what was happening to such bequests to cause the Council to refuse to open its books to the Commission for Charitable Purposes in 1655). Hopes of economic recovery were pinned on improved communications with the port of Bristol, and both Parliament and Lord Protector Cromwell were petitioned several times for powers to make the Avon navigable but without success; Bath was not to get its Bill until 1712. In fact, the petitions put them in an even worse case for they were expensive and the Council had to resort to letting the Common, at £110 per annum, after persuading the commoners to give up their interests 'for as long as necessary'.

The City put on a show for the Restoration, with claret in the conduits and the customary troop of virgins, 400 of them, carrying crowns and garlands in 'all manner of rare and choicest flowers', and another for the Coronation with wine, beer, bread, cakes, and £4 10s od of fireworks which melted the lead on two roofs, but by 1664 the Council was selling off houses to 'put the Chamber out of debt' and had resorted to the desperate measure of reducing the Mayor's stipend to £22 and allowing him only one feast. The Mayor still had his pride, however, for two years later Joan Sperring was thrown out of St Catharine's Hospital and deprived of her black gown for using 'very lowde and scurrilous language' to Mrs Joan Pearce, the Mayor's wife.

Change of Government naturally produced change at local level. Three members of Council who had been removed during the Parliamentary period were given writs of restitution and their replacements were dismissed. Prynne, who had been 'disabled' by Parliament for proclaiming Charles II in 1652, was returned to office in place of James Ash of Freshford, while Ash and Harington were replaced by Popham and Prynne as MPs. The election of the two latter turned out to be a lively affair. One of the reinstated councillors was Captain Henry Chapman who had been Deputy-Governor when the City was held for the King. He was incensed at the proposal to elect two men who had served Parliament and proposed his old superior, Sir Thomas Bridges, now a Deputy Lieutenant of the county whom the Corporation was suing for extortion. Bridges in his turn accused the Mayor, John Ford, of disloyalty and had him summoned before the Privy Council, sending the warrant to Chapman who ordered the constables to serve it publicly 'to disgrace the Mayor'. While Ford was in London Chapman called the Council together and proposed Bridges and Sir Maurice Berkeley as MPS but the Mayor, fully exonerated, returned earlier than expected and called a counter-election, at which Chapman left the Guildhall and had a drum beaten round the town to call in the freemen to vote. After which he dispensed ale with such liberality that many got drunk, 'to the great disturbance of the peace of the said City'. The idea that all the freemen and not just the Council had the right to vote for MPS was not legally sound and although Chapman tried to beat his drum again, he had lost his case.

This all happened in March. In September the Mayoral election came up and Chapman, who wanted the office, could not command enough votes. Nothing deterred, he hit on the happy idea of kidnapping four aldermen and five councillors to even things up, and his friends Bridges and Berkeley issued the necessary warrants for securing them. Having safely incarcerated the opposition in Devizes the would-be Mayor found he had miscalculated, so he seized two more, and then, by voting for himself, managed to secure an 11–10 majority. Ford and Prynne, however, pointed out that the other candidate, Parker, had been nominated by eight of the absentees whose votes could thus be included. Once again Chapman had lost, and this time the Council called him to account. He refused to appear and the bailiffs who were sent to arrest him were fined £10 each for failing to secure him.

The result was that the King received two counter-petitions, one from Ford and one from Chapman, a circumstance which he considered 'a bad example to other corporations', as well he might. Charles took away Chapman's commission in the Militia and confirmed that Parker was mayor. He also suggested that a loyal gift might be

appropriate, and in consequence Prynne presented him with
£100 in gold 'in his Privy Chamber at Whitehall'. Chapman,
however, was irrepressible and on 22 October 1663 his
fellow-councillors elected him their Mayor.

In the same year, on 8 September, Charles II wrote to
Clarendon: 'My wife is well pleased with the bath and finds
herself in very good temper after it, and I hope the effect
will be as she desires, and so God keep you.' Catharine's
desire, to have a child, was not fulfilled, but Bath claimed a
success with the next Queen, Mary of Modena, for in the
year following the Court visit of 1687, she gave birth to a
son, the future Old Pretender, an event so unexpected and
so disturbing to the hopes of a Protestant succession that
the opposition put it about that the baby had been smuggled
into the bed in a warming pan.

Antagonism to James II, which centred on his Roman
Catholicism, was not official policy in Bath. In 1679 they
had already dismissed Alderman Hicks for 'scandalous
words against HRH the Duke of York', and when Monmouth, the illegitimate but Protestant son of Charles II,
called upon the city to help him, during the ill-fated and
tragic rebellion of 1685, they rejected him, shot one of his
soldiers dead and sent a message to the King saying that
'our loyal resolution being so resolutely fixed . . . we had
resolved to die at the gates, rather than suffer him to get
within them'. Fine words, but according to Judge Jeffries
there had been traitors within, and the sheriff sent word that
the council were to

erect a gallows to hang the aforesaid traitors on . . .
halters to hang them with, a sufficient number of faggots
to burn the bowels of four traitors, and a furnace or
cauldron to boil their heads and quarters (and an axe or
cleaver for the quartering) and salt to boil therewith, half
a bushel to each traitor, and tar to tar them with, and a
sufficient number of spears and poles to fix and place
their heads and quarters.

This savage do-it-yourself execution kit is part of the story of the Bloody Assizes which made Jeffries the most hated man in Somerset history.

Whatever private feelings may have been, official Bath remained stubbornly and demonstratively loyal to whatever government was in power, and when James fled from England and William of Orange, 'Dutch Billy', landed on 5 November 1688 the Bath bells rang and there was great rejoicing. For the coronation on 11 April 1689 a hundred young men carried naked swords and once again virgins were assembled, some of them dressed in Amazonian costume which a Victorian writer surmised 'must have been more noticeable than decent'. 'God save King William and Queen Mary; let their enemies perish', proclaimed their banner. The procession banqueted at the Guildhall, and the night was spent in dancing. In an unaccustomed burst of Protestant zeal the Council ordered the Crown of Thorns and Cross in the Cross Bath to be taken down and the inscription obliterated.

Loyalty was further expressed in the reception given to Princess Anne and her husband George of Denmark in 1692, but to the consternation of the Council their demonstration aroused the anger of the Queen who was at loggerheads with her sister, mainly over Anne's friendship with the Marlboroughs and her private application to Parliament for a personal income. 'Sir', read the Mayor,

> The Queen has been informed that yourself and your brethren have attended the Princess with the same respect and ceremony as have usually been paid to the Royal family. Perhaps you have not heard what occasion her Majesty has had to be displeased with the Princess; and therefore I am commanded to acquaint you, that you are not for the future to pay her Highness any such respect of ceremony, without leave from her Majesty, who does not doubt of receiving from you and your brethren this public mark of your duty.

Fortunately, Anne was sympathetic to them in their pre-
dicament, and waived further ceremony.

It was not, however, for the compliments of the Corporation that people came to the City but for the hope of healing
offered by the waters, and although the Chamberlain's
accounts are heavy laden with the cost of hospitality, of gifts
of wine and beer and sugar ('Doble Refined Loffe' sugar for
Richard Cromwell), and plate (£31 10s for a 'Bason and
Eure' for Queen Mary), a much greater proportion of
entries are concerned with the repair and improvement of
the Baths. The biggest single item of expenditure in the
century was £150 4s 8d for 'building the cross in the
King's Bath', probably the elaborate erection shown in
Johnson's drawing of 1675. The Council also concerned
itself with general amenities, frequently repairing and
improving the water supply to the conduits and 'feathers',
the branches to houses, which were a source of revenue,
constructing a number of sewers ('shoars') and providing
public lavatories ('Houses of Ease'), planting trees in 'the
Green', occasionally cleaning the streets, railing the 'Burrow
walls' to provide a walk, setting out part of the Town
Common for 'gentlemen's coaches and horses to take the
air', and repairing the 'waies'.

It is difficult, especially in view of our present standards of
hygiene, to assess the efficacy of their efforts, but the comments of two shrewd contemporary observers are not
unfavourable. In 1668 Samuel Pepys having, with some
difficulty, begged leave from the Admiralty, visited his
parents and then made a trip to the West with his wife, who
was a Somerset woman. He spent two days in Bath and wrote
that the town was 'most of stone, and clean, though the
streets generally narrow', the baths 'pleasant . . . and the
manner pretty enough, only methinks it cannot be clean to
go so many bodies together in the same water', and the music
'extraordinary good as ever I heard at London almost, or
anywhere: 5s'. In King William's time, in 1695, came Celia
Fiennes, the intrepid, emancipated, clear-eyed daughter of

Nat Fiennes, the man who had surrendered Bristol to Prince
Rupert. In her *Journal* she noted that 'the streets are of
good size and well pitched. There are several good houses
built for lodgings that are new and adorned, and good
furniture.' Neither Sam nor Celia complained about behaviour at the Baths, although Pepys noted that 'The King's
and Queen's [were] full of a mixed sort, good and bad, and
Cross only almost for gentry', which suggests considerable
recent improvements if we are to believe a writer in 1634 who
remarked that to see

> all kinde of Persons, of all Shapes, and Formes, of all
> Degrees of all Countryes, and of all Diseases, of both
> Sexes . . . appeare so nakedly, and fearfully, in their
> uncouth, naked Postures, would a little astonish, and putt
> one in mind of the Resurrection.

The detailed description Celia Fiennes gives of visiting
the baths indicates reasonable decorum. There are male
guides in the water for men, female guides for the ladies,
and the serfes 'keep their due distance'. There is a 'serjeant'
who 'takes notice order is preserved and punishes the rude'
for which he 'deserves his reward at the end of the season'.
Ladies wear a yellow canvas gown which the water fills up
'so that your shape is not seen' and the gentlemen wear
drawers and waistcoats of the same material. Celia used one
of the doors and 'slips' from the water and described the
prudish process in some detail. The door descended some
way into the water and when you were through you continued to wade up the steps. As you rose, dripping, a
'garment of flannel' was flung over your head and the guides
pulled it down and removed your bath gown at the same time
so that you were always covered. Then your nightgown
and slippers were put on and you were carried in a chair,
lined with red baize which made it 'close and warm',
right into your bedroom. When this happened to Pepys
he then sweated in bed for an hour, after two hours in the
water.

Celia also noted the customs of drinking the water, which tasted like 'the water that boils eggs', and of being 'pumped' in the King's Bath, on the legs for lameness and on the head for palsies; head-pumping was taken in a broad-brimmed hat with the crown cut out 'so as the brim cast off the water from the face'. The baths, which had gravel bottoms, were, she says, emptied and refilled twice a day, once after the morning bathe and once at night, and it was important to have the white scum cleaned off the surface or the bather was likely to break out into the 'Bath mantle' of 'heat and pimples'.

Neither writer mentioned any place of indoor assembly, for the simple reason that none existed. The bowling greens and tennis courts continued and the visitor could stroll among the trees of the Green (now the Orange Grove) or along the walks in Kingsmead but there was no Pump Room, no Assembly Rooms, and apart from a very occasional ball in the cramped quarters of the old Guildhall nothing to attract the indoor pleasure-seeker. At the end of the seventeenth century Bath was a resort with a national reputation for its healing waters, a decent enough City, capable of handling the seasonal influx of poor and middle-class patients and tourists and the occasional visit of Royalty, but a small place of some 3,000 souls confined within its medieval walls except for a modest extension down Southgate Street and along the London Road. In the next 100 years it was to become a national rendezvous for Society, and to grow at such a rate that in the first national Census of 1801 it is recorded as having a population of 34,160, the eighth largest city in England.

Such development deserves attention, but what is of particular importance is that it took place at a time when a splendid building stone and a remarkable architectural spirit combined to create a unique townscape of international importance, a lesson and delight to anyone who has concern for the human environment. In the eighteenth century there was created in Bath, in response to certain economic demands, a new city of outstanding beauty on a human scale which inspires deep affection. The problems this sets for a changed economy in any age of different technology will be considered later but for the moment we must see something of how Georgian Bath came to be.

7 *Boom Town*
The Eighteenth Century

On 26 April 1708, the year the nation rejoiced in Marlborough's victory at Oudenarde, the Corporation of Bath resolved to sell the town oxen, plough, and harness with all convenient speed. The last symbolic link between town and country had been cut, and the City was embarked on a tide of events which was to sweep it into a unique, totally urban, exotic, and eventually urbane situation, a tide which the Corporation had neither the power, inclination or ability to control. The Council was not noticeably inefficient or corrupt, although there is perhaps some hint of malpractice in a minute of 7 April 1731 which stated that in future no new work over £5 was to be started without a majority vote, that the Mayor might not authorise Tavern Scores except on official business, and that no Chamberlain could be elected Mayor until his accounts had been passed. We can hardly take the charge against an alderman in 1740 of being involved in a 'Sodemiticall Attempt' as evidence of general moral depravity.

In their limited way, the Corporation continued to do useful work in connection with the baths and streets. The occasional sewer was authorised, improvements were made to walks by the walls, a Pump House was put up in 1713, rebuilt in 1732, enlarged in 1734 and given a marble cistern instead of a copper one in 1735. Land was leased in the

Bridewell in 1721 for a Charity School for boys and girls (Nelson's Blue Coat school, founded in 1711) which was rebuilt in neo-Jacobean style by Manners and Gill in 1859 and is now Council offices, and in 1744 the Corporation paid £550 for the Black Swan in Broad Street where in 1752 they built a new King Edward's school to plans of Thomas Jelly, a handsome building still to be seen. They continued to look after the water supply, did something about street lighting, and at the instigation of Dr Bave, a German settled in Bath, bought a fire engine which did sterling service at a conflagration in Queen Square in 1746. They even took some concern with public morals, insisting in 1737 that 'no Male person over 10 was to bathe without a Pair of Drawers and a Waistcoat, and no Female person without a Decent Shift' – male Guides also had to wear a tasselled cap. In 1753 they tried to stop mixed bathing but had to rescind the order a fortnight later and be content with a ban on mixed *swimming*.

Nor was the Corporation without some interest and influence in building. It is true that, when in 1727 John Wood offered to reconstruct their city 'in a regular manner', the majority considered his plan 'chimerical' and turned it down. But Wood himself, who normally could see little of virtue in other men's work, acknowledged in 1734 that the Defects seemed 'on the point of decreasing' and, although the grandest and best-known bits of Georgian planning lie outside the old city, the medieval buildings did in fact disappear, in a piecemeal process which gave it a rather charming irregularity. By 1757 the Corporation had woken to the need for more drastic action and was preparing to petition for the Act which when they eventually got it in 1789 enabled them to carry out a most attractive reconstruction of the Baths and the area around. Preoccupation with the curative attractions of the town, however, caused them to miss the importance of a new magnetic force in Bath. When in 1745 the Mayor greeted Princess Caroline at the North Gate with the statement, 'Other Parts of the

Kingdom may be better situated to serve his Majesty in Traffic and Revenue; but it is the peculiar Happiness of BATH to preserve the lives of his illustrious Family', he omitted to mention a Traffic and Revenue which while not enriching the Throne certainly enriched many private individuals – the commerce of the card table.

Wood, writing in 1742, marked the visit of Queen Anne in 1702 as the event which initiated the meteoric rise of Bath as a resort for the fashionable world. The Court was, in fact, rapidly ceasing to be the centre of Society, and what this visit, and the second one in the following year, achieved was to focus attention on Bath at a time when, as Goldsmith said, people of fashion 'wanted some place where they might have each other's company and win each other's money, as they had during the winter in town'. The result was a city crammed with chaos, a dangerous and dissolute place with surly servants and rapacious chairmen, oafish ruffians and professional bullies, where tempers flared and quarrels were settled with the sword. The Corporation tried to meet fire with fire and appointed as Master of Ceremonies a dissolute bully and gambler, one Captain Webster. He did not improve matters and the solution was to come from a man of very different temperament who took the basic life of baths, balls, and betting, shot through with scandal and seduction, and, by the sheer force of his personality and power of organisation, forced it into a mould of manners which was to be a pattern for the nation. Such was the remarkable achievement of Richard 'Beau' Nash, the uncrowned King of Bath.

He was born at Swansea, in 1674, the son of a glass manufacturer, who sent him to Carmarthen Grammar School and thence to Oxford, where he lasted four terms before he left for reasons variously reported but probably involving female entanglement. His father then bought him 'a pair of colours' in the Guards but Richard did not find the life to his liking, sold his commission, and enrolled in the Inner Temple where he became a leader of the smart set and appears to have supported himself mainly by gambling and presents from women, for unspecified services. His impressive bearing, self-confidence, and sartorial finery, which were later to stand him in good stead as 'King' of Bath had already earned him the nickname of 'the Count' and it was 'the Count' who was chosen in 1695 to organise the pageant to be presented to the new King, William of Orange.

This was a great success and William offered him a knighthood but apparently Nash asked to be a 'Knight of Windsor', which carried a pension, and nothing came of it. For another ten years Nash continued his social life in London and then in 1705, at the age of 31, his need for money brought him to Bath where he is reputed to have won £1,000 in his first season, and where his qualities caused Webster to offer him a job as gentleman-in-waiting. Shortly afterwards Webster was killed in a duel in the Grove and Nash accepted the unpaid post of Master of Ceremonies. So started a reign which was to last for over half a century.

It was probably due to Nash that the Corporation built a new Pump Room, designed by John Harvey, and it was Nash who engaged musicians from London. There was already a small theatre, built by George Trim for £1,300 on the site of the present Royal Mineral Water Hospital, and another, 'The Globe', near Westgate where the Bath Company of Comedians played. A Cold Bath House (demolished 1966) was built in Claverton Street by Thomas Greenaway in 1707. What was particularly needed was an adequate public room for dances and gaming, and in 1708 Nash persuaded Thomas Harrison to build an Assembly Room near the present North Parade overlooking ground by the Avon which became known as Harrison's Walks. A ballroom and portico were added in 1720 by William Killigrew who Wood dismissed as 'a Joiner, who laid his Apron aside about 1719', and the whole building was remodelled in 1749. It was burnt down in 1820, rebuilt for the Royal Literary Institution and demolished finally in 1933.

Apparently Harrison used his monopoly to raise charges so Nash negotiated with Humphrey Thayer, a London apothecary who had made considerable property investments in Bath, for a second Assembly Room opposite the first. This was designed by John Wood and opened in 1730 with Dame Lindsey as lessee. It was pulled down in the nineteenth century to make way for York Street. When Harrison died Nash gave permission for Dame Lindsey to install her sister, Mrs Haynes, in his place, but this re-established the monopoly and Nash had to intervene to keep prices down. Mrs Haynes, having made a fortune, married Lord Hawley. She also acquired the old 'play-room' of George Trim, but this was not profitable. Attendance was poor and the maximum take was £30. When the site was needed for the hospital in 1738 the theatre moved to a cellar in Simpson's Assembly Rooms (as Harrison's now was). This also was inadequate and in 1747 an actor, John Hippisley, proposed that a new one should be built. The idea was taken up by John Palmer, a wealthy brewer and chandler, father of the John Palmer of mail coach fame, and building was started in 1747 in Orchard Street to a design probably by Thomas Jelly. The exterior can still be seen, but the interior was twice re-modelled. In 1767 the Corporation successfully petitioned for a licence for 'Mr Palmer's Theatre in Orchard Street' and Bath obtained the first Theatre Royal in the provinces. It had a generally successful history, including the appearance of the young Sarah Siddons from 1778, one of her earliest roles being that of Mrs Candour in *School for Scandal*. The site was not, however, very convenient, especially as Bath was growing northwards, and in 1805 a new Theatre Royal was opened in Beaufort Square, built by another John Palmer to designs by George Dance the younger which are today in the Soane Museum. The old front can still be seen facing the square, but the rest was rebuilt to a design by C. J. Phipps after a disastrous fire in 1862.

The 'Lower Rooms', as they were called after the opening of the 'Upper Rooms' (the present Assembly Rooms) in 1771, were not only the places where a brilliant, if smelly, company would gather for breakfasts and balls,* but were for the first half of the century crowded with gamblers both male and female, for Nash had made it a fashionable pastime for the ladies. Nash, although a professional gambler, was not renowned for very large winnings and it is probably from the beginning, as it was certain at the end, that he derived a considerable income from a share in the house profits. It is difficult to see how otherwise he could have maintained his great state, with fine clothes, gilt coach and six horses, large house in St John's Court (now the 'Garrick's Head'), fine furnishings, and 'a whore in the house', not to mention his stakes at the table. 'Would you think it, my lord,' he is reported as saying 'that damned bitch Fortune no later than last night, tricked me out of five hundred! It is not surprising that my luck should never turn – that I should thus eternally be mauled?' 'I don't wonder at your losing money,' said his friend, Chesterfield, 'but all the world is surprised where you get it to lose.'

The gambling craze died out and with it Nash's fortune. In 1739 an Act was passed to prevent excessive and fraudulent gambling and it suppressed all private lotteries and games of Faro, Basset, Hazard, and Ace of Hearts. The fine was £20 – one-third to the informer and the rest, if the offence was in Bath, to the new hospital. After a temporary setback there was a revival with new games not mentioned in the law of which the chief was EO (Even and Odd) invented in Nash's other empire, Tunbridge Wells. This was a form of roulette where the divisions were marked alternately E and O, the proprietors having two bar holes which gave them an advantage of five per cent. These

---

* Philip Thicknesse (*New Prose Bath Guide*, 1778) was appalled. 'We really think that the Wit of Man could not contrive a more certain Method to defeat the Efficacy of all Medicine, or endanger the Lives of those who come to Bath for their Health, than attending a Dress Ball in a full season.'

innovations were made illegal by an Act of 1745 which brought about the end of public gambling until the present-day revival. There would, of course, have been illegal establishments, and in 1749 the Corporation paid 1s for faggots 'to burn Little Dick's EO table'.

EO (or OE) did some damage to Nash, permanently to his purse and temporarily to his reputation. He found that he was getting nothing like his full rake-off and he took Wiltshire (who had succeeded Dame Lindsey) to court. He lost the action as it was ruled that the contract was immoral, but Wiltshire was also sued by the vestry of St Peter and St Paul (the Abbey) for keeping a gaming-house, and was fined £500. Deprived of his main source of income, Nash, an old man now, was forced to sell off most of his finery and move into the smaller house next door. Friends helped, particularly in subscribing to his non-existent book on Bath and Tunbridge Wells – even the Corporation voted £52 10s in 1755 for 25 copies, but they did not get round to giving him a pension until 1760, the year before he died, and at ten guineas a month it was hardly generous.

In his last ten years the ageing Beau continued to exert a now rather capricious control over the social life and he commanded respect chiefly for his past achievements and his great age for the social background of his triumphs was passing away, and he himself had become something of a bore. And yet there was still some power of personality left. In 1752 the white marble statue which still stands was erected in the Pump Room and was paid for, as Fielding wrote, 'by several of the principal inhabitants of this place out of gratitude for his well-known prudent management for about forty years, with regard to the regulations of the diversions, the accommodations of persons, resorting hither, and the general good of the city', and in the same year Lady Luxborough wrote to the poet Shenstone:

Would you see our law-giver, Mr Nash, whose white hat commands more respect and non-resistance than the crown of some kings, though now worn on a head that is in its eightieth year of age? To promote good society, good manners, and a coalition of parties and ranks; to suppress scandal and late hours are his views; and he succeeds better than his brother monarchs usually do.

Religious enthusiasts were less kind. 'As long as you roll in a continual circle of sensual delights and vain entertainments,' wrote one, 'you are dead to all the purposes of pity and virtue. You are as odious to God as a corrupt carcase that lies putrifying in the churchyard.'

On the night of 12 February 1761, the old Beau passed away in his house in Saw Close and all Bath mourned. He had a fine funeral for which the Corporation contributed a sum 'not exceeding fifty guineas', and after lying in state for four days his body was carried to the Abbey for burial. The chief mourners were Mr Wiltshire and Mr Simpson, the Masters of the Assembly Rooms, who were followed by several members of the Corporation, the beadles of the Hospital, and the poor patients. The procession was headed by the boys and girls of the charity schools. Eight days later the Corporation accepted William Hoare's offer of a portrait of Nash to hang in the Town Hall, but nine years were to pass before an Abbey monument was erected, the subscription for which was raised by Dr Henry Harington, who himself composed the inscription to the 'Elegentiae Arbiter'. Of all the panegyrics published we can see most truth in that by his friend, the decent and intelligent Dr Oliver, physician to the Hospital and inventor of the famous Bath Oliver biscuit. He acknowledged the Beau's 'faults and foibles' – 'his passions were strong; which, as they fired him to act strenuously in good, hurried him to some excess in evil' – but he also emphasised his great kindness and concern for 'the young, the gay and heedless fair, just launching upon the dangerous seas of pleasure'. Indeed there must have been many who remembered the departed despot with affection and, with Christopher Anstey, hoped that:

15 Richard Nash, from a portrait of 1746

16 (*overleaf*) North Parade and Lower Assembly Rooms.
Watercolour by Thomas Malton

17 Rosewell House, before cleaning

In reward of his Labours, his Virtue, and Pains,
He is footing it now in th'Elysian Plains,
Indulg'd as a token of Prosperpine's Favour,
To preside at her Balls in a Cream-colour'd Beaver.

Nash was proud of his friendship with princes, but he was not a snob. The Corporation might grovel, kiss hands, and present freedoms in gold boxes (silver for the lesser nobility), but Nash met distinguished visitors on an equal footing – even a superior one, for they were entering his kingdom. 'One more dance, Mr Nash,' cried the imperious Amelia in 1728, 'remember I am a Princess!' 'Yes, madam,' answered Nash, 'but I reign here, and my laws must be kept.' And so they were, and all were equal before them so that strangers could meet and classes mingle without awkwardness. As Wood wrote, 'When proper Walks were made for exercise and a House built for assembling in, Rank began to be laid aside, and all Degrees of People, from the Private Gentleman upwards, were soon united in Society with one another.' For a brief period there was, above a certain class, an Open Society bound by a single passion, gaming, and a single law, the rule of Nash. No wonder it met such virulent opposition from religious men and women who sought a similar situation but with a different passion and a different law.

According to Goldsmith, Nash 'was the first who diffused a desire for society and an easiness of address among a whole people, who were formerly censured by foreigners for a reservedness of behaviour and an awkward timidity in their first approaches' and from Bath this new openness spread so that 'the whole kingdom became more refined by lessons originally derived from him'. A large claim, but not without some substance, even if not everyone approved of the new ways. The redoubtable Sarah Churchill wrote in 1716 to Lady Cowper that Her Grace of Shrewsbury was 'as well pleased in a great Crowd of Strangers as the common People are with Bull-baiting or a Mountebank' but that she herself had 'been upon the Walks but twice, and never saw any Place Abroad that had more Stinks and Dirt in it than Bath'. Admittedly there was 'a great Plenty of Meat' but the Noise kept her awake and she would bear it only as long as she thought the waters were doing the Duke some good. This did not prevent her spending a good deal of time at the tables and becoming friendly with Nash to whom she often wrote for advice about her great house building at Blenheim.

The daily routine, described at some length by Goldsmith, was hardly exhilarating. On arrival the visitor was greeted by a peal of bells and the town waits. This meant half-a-guinea to the ringers and half-a-crown to the singers. Then the subscriptions were taken out – two guineas at the Assembly Rooms for balls and music; half-a-crown to a guinea for the walks;* 5s to a guinea to a lending library; coffee-house subscriptions for pen, ink, and paper for letter-writing; possibly a reading-room subscription, and another for one of the proprietary chapels.

A morning started with bathing between 6 and 9 followed by a general assembly in the Pump Room for a chat, three glasses of water, and music. Then to the separate male and female coffee houses and afterwards to breakfast which was most likely in public at the Assembly Room accompanied by a concert or a 'breakfast lecture' where the arts and sciences were taught 'in a pretty superficial manner, so as not to tease the understanding, while they afford the imagination some amuzement'. Towards noon the visitor could go to the Abbey, an activity encouraged by Nash, take a walk, read in a booksellers, or make arrangements for the evening. A hearty dinner was then eaten in lodgings, after which the company met again in the Pump Room before going out to the walks and to take tea in the Assembly Rooms.

The evenings were spent in visiting, or at the theatre, the gambling table, or the ball, usually held on Tuesdays and

* I.e. Harrison's Walk. Later the Spring Gardens on the opposite side of the river reached by ferry were opened about 1740 and remained until 1796. Its site is now largely covered by Johnstone Street.

Fridays and conducted with extreme formality. Carried to the Assembly Rooms by the now officially licensed chairmen charging fixed rates,* the company would assemble round the room, the elder ladies and children being content, according to Mr Nash's Rules, with the second bench, 'as being past or not yet come to perfection'. The dancing started at 6 and the first two hours were given up to the minuet, danced by only one couple at a time, each gentleman dancing with two ladies in succession –

> Now why should I mention a hundred or more
> Who went the same circle as others before,
> To a tune that they played a hundred times o'er?
>
> (Anstey, *New Bath Guide*, 1766)

Why indeed! Affairs livened up a little with the country dances which followed but things were very different from the rowdy days when the men had trampled around in their boots and spurs and the women followed the milkmaid fashion of wearing aprons – all forbidden by Nash. There was a break for supper at 9 and then country dances continued until at the stroke of 11 the music was stopped by Nash, who employed the musicians. 'The order,' wrote Goldsmith, 'the decorum, the measured pomp, that distinguished the festivities of Bath were the pride and boast of the place.'

The year 1734, when Nash was 60, probably marks the height of his power and achievement. In this year came the ugly but amiable Prince of Orange, who benefited from the waters and gave Nash a gold snuff box. In his honour the Grove was renamed the Orange Grove and Nash caused an

---

* Sixpence ($2\frac{1}{2}$p) for any distance within the city, another sixpence for up to 500 yards outside the baths, and 1s for a mile. The Chairmen to stop as often as required but not more than ten minutes in a 6d fare and 20 minutes in a 1s fare. If longer, they could charge at 6d a half hour. There was a fine of 10s for swearing at the passenger, but passengers were liable to a fine if they refused to pay their fare, or defaced the chair. (*Bath and Bristol Guide*, 1755.)

obelisk to be erected there with a Latin inscription celebrating the Prince's recovery which can be more easily read than the one commemorating the monument's repair in 1820. Nash's other obelisk is in Queen Square and was put up in 1738 in honour of Frederick Prince of Wales, who gave the Beau yet another snuff box. Wood designed the monument, which then rose to a sharp point, and was very proud of it. Nash tried to get the famous Alexander Pope, to write a suitable inscription, was snubbed for his pains, but persevered and received a composition so flat as to be insulting.

IN MEMORY

OF HONOURS CONFERR'D

AND IN GRATITUDE

FOR BENEFITS BESTOW'D

IN THIS CITY

BY HIS ROYAL HIGHNESS

FREDERICK

PRINCE OF WALES

AND HIS

ROYAL CONSORT

IN THE YEAR MDCCXXXVIII

THIS OBELISK IS ERECTED

BY RICHARD NASH, ESQ.

Two years later, in 1740, the Corporation honoured Nash by placing a full-length portrait of him in Wiltshire's Rooms between the busts of Pope and Newton, which provoked an anonymous sneer in *The Gentleman's Magazine*:

Immortal NEWTON never spoke,
More truth than here you'll find,
Nor POPE himself e'er penned a joke
Severer on mankind.

The picture plac'd the busts between
Gives satire all its strength;
Wisdom and Wit are little seen,
But Folly at full length.

This is unfair to Nash and it is a pity that simplified sentiments are often more memorable than the complicated truth. Not only was Nash's transformation of Bath society a real, remarkable, and necessary achievement, not only did many have cause to remember with gratitude his kindness, but 'folly' was put to considerable public service when Nash was organising publicity and raising money for the new General Hospital (now the Royal Mineral Water Hospital). He contributed £100 himself and even got 40 guineas out of tight-fisted Sarah Churchill, while in the second subscription list of 1742 we read: 'The King, per Mr Nash £200; the Prince of Wales, do.; the Princess of Wales £50.' Fittingly, his portrait still hangs in the Hospital.

This new hospital was but one unit in the great expansion of building which took place in Bath in the eighteenth century in a style which, like the orderly procession of the social day, was bound by Rules, imposed by the architect John Wood and followed faithfully by his son, and a host of other builders in the town. But whereas Nash made his own system, Wood took his from the Palladian school.

Andrea Palladio (1508–80) was an Italian architect who designed many lovely villas and town houses. He studied Roman architecture both in the antiquities of Italy and in the *De Architectura* of Vitruvius, the only surviving architectural book from Classical times. In 1570 he published in Venice, *I Quattro Libri dell'Architettura*, which included the fruits of his researches, drawings of his own buildings, and rules for designing in terms of the Classical Orders. English editions of this famous book appeared in 1663, 1715, 1736 and 1738.

Palladian principles were brought to England by Inigo Jones (1573–1652) who had visited Italy, learnt the language, and had his own copy of the *Quattro Libri*, but under the influence of Wren (1632–1723) the classical forms of pillar, pediment, and dome found a freer, more daring expression. The turn of the century saw a 'Back to Palladio' movement headed by the enthusiastic and influential

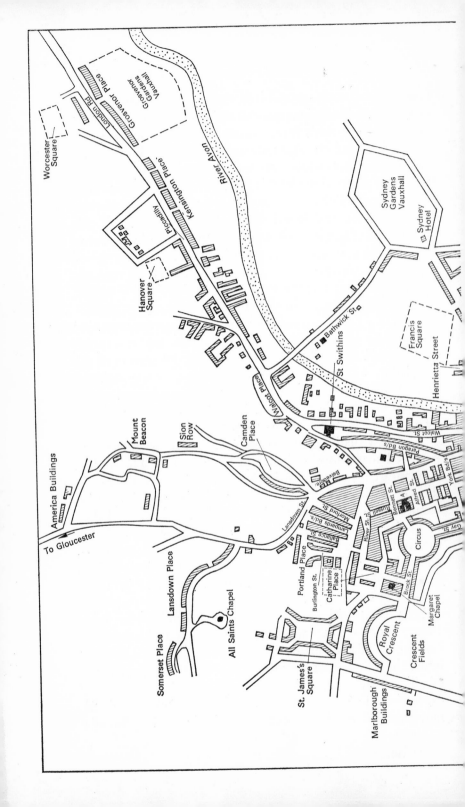

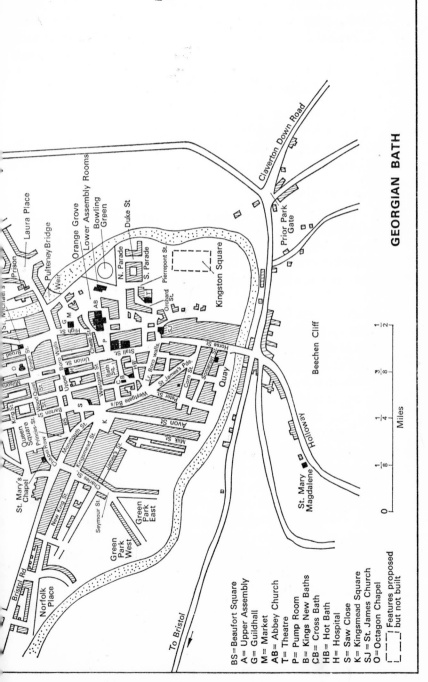

N ←

GEORGIAN BATH

Claverton Down Road

Laura Place

Pulteney Bridge

Weir

Orange Grove

Lower Assembly Rooms

Bowling Green

Duke St

Prior Park Gate

N. Parade

S. Parade

Pierrepont St.

Kingston Square

AB

Orchard St.

High St

G M

P

SJ

Beechen Cliff

Broad St.

St. Michael's

Prison

St. Mary's Chapel

Milsom St.

O

Cheap St.

Corn St.

King St.

Queen Square

Wood Court

Upper Boro Walls

Union St.

Stall St.

Westgate St.

Bath St.

CB

HB

Barton St.

Princes St.

Beaufort Sq.

Trim St.

Westgate Bd's

St. James's Pde.

Horse St.

Peter St.

Avon St.

Corn St.

Somerset St.

Quay

Holloway

St. Mary Magdalene

Norfolk Place

Bristol Rd

New King St.

Seymour St.

Charles St.

James's St.

Kingsmead St.

Monmouth St.

Chapel Row

K

S

Green Park West

Green Park East

Milk St.

To Bristol

Miles

0   1/8   1/4   3/8   1/2

BS = Beaufort Square
A = Upper Assembly
G = Guildhall
M = Market
AB = Abbey Church
T = Theatre
P = Pump Room
B = Kings New Baths
CB = Cross Bath
HB = Hot Bath
H = Hospital
S = Saw Close
K = Kingsmead Square
SJ = St. James Church
O = Octagon Chapel

⌐ ¬ Features proposed
L ⌐ but not built

Richard Boyle, third Earl of Burlington and fifth Earl of Cork, with the architects Colen Campbell, who wrote *Vitruvius Brittanicus* in 1715, and William Kent (1685–1748), designer of the Horse Guards, Whitehall. It became the basic style of early Georgian England and Pope wrote in pro-Palladian terms:

> You too proceed! make falling arts your care,
> Erect new wonders, and the old repair;
> Jones and Palladio to themselves restore,
> And be whate'er Vitruvius was before.

but warned:

> Yet shall (my Lord) your just, your noble rules,
> Fill half the land with imitating Fools.

Fortunately it seems that in that solid age the style was Fool-proof, which is more than can be said for neo-Georgian. What Palladianism did was to lay down rules, and above all rules of proportion so acceptable to the human eye that although one could design an unimaginative building it would be very difficult to produce a downright ugly one. And there was still room for individual genius as a study of the four sides of Queen Square will show.

Superficially, Palladianism may be recognised in Bath by the accentuation of the first floor (the *piano nobile*), the absence of gables, the use of pillars and pilasters, inclusion of pediments, and a general simplicity of ornament which should, wrote Inigo Jones, 'be sollid, proporsionable, according to the rulles, masculine and unaffected'.

The type of building of the pre-Wood era can be seen in the drawings round Gilmore's map of 1694. Very little survives apart from the heavily reconstructed Abbey and the rebuilt Abbey Church House (Hetling House). One or two buildings in Green Street and Broad Street show something of its nature while Brunel's railway station (1840) and the old Blue Coat School (1860) show revivalist attempts at Jacobean façades. The most noticeable characteristics of the earlier period are gables and stone-mullioned windows. Early eighteenth-century non-Wood work shows a change to Classical style but with a much freer, more ornamented treatment. Rosewell House (1736) by Strahan, in Kingsmead Square, is almost Baroque in its swirling forms, and there are houses in Westgate Street and Green Street (1715–20) which while bearing classical columns still have gables and, in some cases, the broken pediments of a slightly earlier period and the swelling bolection mouldings of the early eighteenth century. Shell hoods, typical of the Queen Anne period, can be seen in Green Street and Trim Street. Another feature distinguishing the new building from the old is the use of sash windows, an innovation of the late seventeenth century, although it must be remembered that windows are often the most altered parts of a building. Buildings were also often merely re-faced in the contemporary style and there are houses in Bath in, for example, Lilliput Lane (where Sally Lunn sold her tea-cakes), Abbey Green, and Broad Street which have a Georgian face on a medieval skull.

Wood's great achievement, however, was not so much to introduce a new style for individual buildings but to see the townscape in terms of a planned layout, meeting the demand for individual houses by welding them together into a satisfying whole. The uniformity he imposed, which was not rigid, lay in the façades; behind this there was room for variety to meet individual requirements. He did, however, insist on the use of good materials to a high standard of finish and congratulated himself on having vastly improved on the shoddy conditions of lodgings that had existed before, with the floors made brown 'with soot and small beer to hide the dirt, as well as their own imperfections' and speckled with the 'particular whitewash' used for covering the hearths and chimney pieces.

There was no overall plan for the new Bath, only individual bits of planning, of a high order. What gives it a feeling of cohesion is the use of a common material, a common

idiom, a common scale, and a great sensitivity to the neigh-
bourliness of building to building and town to topography,
a reflection in stone of the varied but cohesive society which
the Beau had made. And it was this spirit, continued for
over a century by a variety of builders, that we owe to John
Wood the Elder.

He was born in 1704, the son of a Bath builder, but we
know very little about his early life except that he became
surveyor-builder to Lord Chancellor Bingley and had
experience in building and landscaping in Yorkshire and
probably in town building in the Grosvenor-Cavendish area
of London. When he saw that the river traffic was being
opened up from Bristol to Bath he turned his mind seriously
to the possibility of building there and in 1725 'formed one
design', as he wrote, 'for the ground on the north-west
corner of the city, and another for the land on the north-east
side of the town and river'. Each area was to have a Royal
Forum for Assembly, a Grand Circus for sports, and an
Imperial Gymnasium, 'for the Practice of medicinal Exer-
cises' (whatever *they* might be!). Wood's historical ideas
were fanciful. What he in fact came to build were mainly
lodging houses and although he managed to fashion one lot
into a Circus it was never used for sports. In November 1725
he fixed preliminary articles with Gay, a surgeon of Hatton
Garden who owned the land to the north-west, and in 1727
he settled in Bath, his son being born in the same year.

His first work was private. The Duke of Chandos, who
had been building near Bingley in Cavendish Square, had
bought up much of the property of St John's Hospital and
wished to build a house for himself and refashion the
hospital to include lodgings for visitors. At first he called in
the Bristol architect, Strahan, who was designing Beaufort
Square, Kingsmead Square, and the now vanished Kingsmead and Avon Street houses, but replaced him by Wood
whom he had managed to detach from Bingley. Thus
Wood's first works in Bath are St John's Hospital and
Chandos Court. In the same year, 1727, he added a fine

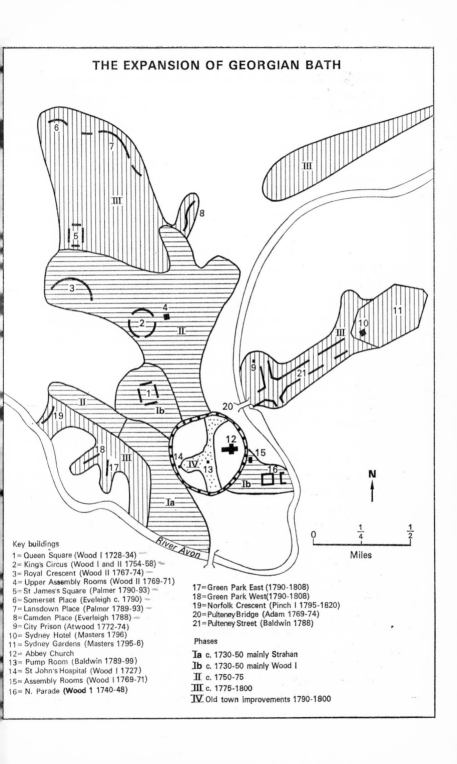

THE EXPANSION OF GEORGIAN BATH

Key buildings

1= Queen Square (Wood I 1728-34)
2= King's Circus (Wood I and II 1754-58)
3= Royal Crescent (Wood II 1767-74)
4= Upper Assembly Rooms (Wood II 1769-71)
5= St James's Square (Palmer 1790-93)
6= Somerset Place (Eveleigh c. 1790)
7= Lansdown Place (Palmer 1789-93)
8= Camden Place (Everleigh 1788)
9= City Prison (Atwood 1772-74)
10= Sydney Hotel (Masters 1796)
11= Sydney Gardens (Masters 1795-6)
12= Abbey Church
13= Pump Room (Baldwin 1789-99)
14= St John's Hospital (Wood I 1727)
15= Assembly Rooms (Wood I 1769-71)
16= N. Parade (Wood 1 1740-48)

17= Green Park East (1790-1808)
18= Green Park West(1790-1808)
19= Norfolk Crescent (Pinch I 1795-1820)
20= Pulteney Bridge (Adam 1769-74)
21= Pulteney Street (Baldwin 1788)

Phases

Ia c. 1730-50 mainly Strahan
Ib c. 1730-50 mainly Wood I
II c. 1750-75
III c. 1775-1800
IV. Old town improvements 1790-1800

N

0   1/4   1/2

Miles

River Avon

extension to Ralph Allen's town house, now almost completely obscured by later building, and the next year built
Lindsey's Rooms, opened, as we have seen, in 1730. But
his grand plans received a set-back, for the death of George I
caused Gay, afraid of political instability, to withdraw his
support. It was then that Wood offered his project for
redesigning the city within its walls and when this was
rejected he decided to go it alone.

Having obtained leases at various stages from Gay, he set
about building Queen Square in 1728 and finished it in
1734. He originally intended to level the ground but this
proved too expensive and what was produced was a grand
palace façade along the north side, a simpler range on the
south, a climbing, repetitive pattern of houses on the east,
and on the west three separate houses, the centre one, where
Dr Oliver came to live, set back from the others. This latter
was pulled down in 1830 and the space crammed with a
large neo-Grecian building by Pinch. It was the home of the
Literary and Scientific Institution and is now the Reference
Library. Wood also built in the south-west, in Chapel Row,
a proprietary chapel of St Mary, destroyed for road-widening
in 1875. Queen Square (after Queen Caroline, wife o
George II) together with Gay Street, leading northward,
were completed in 1734 when Wood was 30. The following
year he planned and started work on Prior Park, Ralph
Allen's great mansion, and in 1738 he began the General
Hospital, giving his services free. It was opened in 1742.

Having begun his grand plan for the north-west Wood
started in 1740 on that for the south-east, although not, as
originally intended, over the river at Bathwick. Instead he
built on 'Batt's Gardens' by Harrison's Walks, a region so
marshy and liable to flood that the buildings had to be raised
high on arches. These buildings faced the North Parade
(Wood's Grand Parade) on one side, the South Parade on
the other (the Royal Forum to the south was never built),
and Pierrepont Street on the west. In the other side of this
street Wood inserted an opening with Tuscan columns

18 The Royal Crescent

19 Queen Square.
Watercolour by
Thomas Malton
1784

20 The Circus.
Watercolour by
John Robert Cozzens

21 'The Knights of Baythe.' Cartoon by William O'Gaarth, 1763

22 Inside the Pump Room in 1784. Watercolour by S. Repton

which leads through into Orchard Street where No. 1, a slightly showy pre-Wood (1739) building has been christened Linley House. Linley and his family were notable contributors to the musical life of eighteenth-century Bath, but he is mainly remembered for his daughter's elopement with Sheridan.

After the Parades, Wood turned back to the north-west development and designed the Circus. He started building in 1754 but in that year he died, at the age of 50, after a long and tedious illness, and the work was completed by his son, John Wood the Younger. The elder Wood had made quite a few enemies and a good deal of money.* His building developments were personal business enterprises for which he was planner, developer, salesman, and architect – and he ran a profitable trade in building materials on the side. He had more than a local reputation and outside commissions included restoration at Llandaff Cathedral (1732–52), Bristol Corn Exchange (1741), and Liverpool Town Hall (1749–54). In 1749 he was made a JP for Somerset, but was never a Freeman of Bath. He left a superb legacy of architecture to the city and a son who was at least his equal in skill.

The younger Wood not only finished the Circus, which then surrounded a paved centre, with a reservoir in the centre, but he built Brock Street, named after his father-in-law, to the west and added to it the incomparable Royal Crescent (1767–74), the first of this form in England. Facing the Common, it had uninterrupted views to the south. Other extensions he made to the west were Rivers Street (c. 1770) and the unpretentiously satisfying Catharine Place (c. 1780), but it was to the east of the Circus that the main building took place.

Fashionable Bath was moving northward and its social needs were met by the building of the New or Upper

---

* Rates in the old town charged about 5s and in the top town about 12s (15s or 18s 9d in the Circus).

Assembly Rooms by Wood II from 1769–71. They cost some £20,000 to the shareholders in the tontine (a tontine was an arrangement whereby on the death of a subscriber his shares were distributed amongst the other, so that the last survivor would get all). Basically two rectangular blocks, with an octagonal Card Room added in 1777, the building impresses by its simple external grandeur (a more splendid scheme by Robert Adam was rejected as too expensive) and excites by its interior magnificence. The inside is, however, a reconstruction by Sir A. Richardson, for the building was gutted by fire during the German 'Baedeker' raid of 1942, and while satisfying our historical sense we may perhaps note the fireplaces in a centrally-heated building, tap the hollow 'marble' columns, and consider the acoustics, wondering if perhaps the spirit of Wood would have approved a modern design. Or would he have winced at the incongruity?

Building in this north-east area of Walcot New Town went on apace, not only by Wood but also, in a less severe style, by Atwood (d. 1775), Palmer (1738–1817), Jelly (mid-eighteenth century), and to a lesser extent Baldwin (1750–1820) and Eveleigh (late eighteenth century). Atwood's most notable contribution was the Paragon (1769) which curves its way along the hill, its backside propped up by a cliff of masonry. The principal rooms are downstairs at the back, with views over the Avon valley. Atwood, a wealthy plumber, was a member of the Council and the Paragon was built on Corporation land. Another Corporation concern was the building of Milsom Street which linked the centre of the town with the northern development. The architect is not known for certain but was probably Atwood and/or Jelly.

Daniel Milsom, a wine cooper, had rented the Town Acre, north of the present George Street, in 1755, thus extending Milsom's Gardens, a large tract to the south. Here was a piece of property ripe for development, an open space in the midst of the northward expansion of the city. Unfortunately Milsom seems to have had trouble in letting because of the presence of a Poor House and he applied several times to have his rent 'abated'. The Corporation offered to dock £10 off the £100 per annum, a proposal which Milsom rejected, and in 1760 they came to an agreement whereby they should work together, Milsom to have 'all rents and profits' for 35 years and then to hand over the whole undertaking. In 1762 an advertisement appeared for 99-year leases at 4s-a-foot frontage.

This fine, broad Palladian street, effectively closed and focused on the north by Edgar Buildings on the Town Acre, has seen a number of significant changes. In 1782 the Poor House land became available and Somersetshire Buildings, designed by Baldwin, was inserted in the space, intruding successfully, a later, more decorative Classical style, and breaking the line with pavilions and a bow. Then in the nineteenth century the road was widened by moving back the pavements over the open areas before the buildings which thus lost their railings. Two monumental banks (1865 and 1875) were built at the northern corners, and a little later (*c.* 1904) a classical building with a modest riot of carving covered the passage which led to the Octagon. The latter was a proprietary chapel designed by Lightholer in 1767. This charming and unusual building, whose dome makes it acoustically abominable, fell upon evil days, and was rescued by the Corporation who have recently redecorated and re-floored it. The Victorians put in a stained glass window which was subsequently removed and has unfortunately been reinstated.

The biggest alteration to Milsom Street came from a change in function. Originally residential, in fact mainly lodging houses, it was transformed in the early nineteenth century into a high-class shopping street. This produced a frill of bow windows until the march of progress in the form of steel beams and plate glass substituted flat slabs, a transition which is not however unpleasing as the scale of the street is big enough to absorb it. There are signs that yet another change, this time to offices, is taking place, alarming some of the retailers, and it is possible that we may see a further development in the scene. The most pleasant change, however, would be to remove the parked cars.

Down in the old city the only work by Wood was a new Hot Bath (now the Old Royal Baths). His plans for this were exhibited in 1775 and in 1778 he received £100 from the Corporation for the work. He died in 1781, aged 54, and was buried in Swainswick. In many ways he added more to the urban scene than his father had done, but he was a quieter, less spectacular person and this is reflected in the newspaper notice which simply reports: 'Saturday last . . . died at Batheaston, John Wood Esq., many years one of His Majesty's Justices of the Peace for this County, and well known for his great skill in architecture.'

Wood had also been concerned, along with Atwood, Lightholer, Jelly, Palmer, and Baldwin in the curious story of the new Guildhall. In 1760 it was resolved to replace the old Guildhall, reputedly by Inigo Jones, which in spite of improvements in 1726 was lacking in facilities and occupied an 'incommodious' position in the middle of the High Street. Ralph Allen donated £500, the Corporation sought professional advice and studied plans from Lightholer, Wood and Richard Jones, one-time Clerk of Works to Ralph Allen and now City Surveyor (d. 1766). It is a little uncertain which plan was finally accepted, although they certainly asked Lightholer to provide drawings and a model, for 'not less than £100'. All this took eight years and once the foundation stone was laid in 1768, accompanied by a guinea's worth of bell-ringing from the Abbey, it was another five years before the Corporation put out tenders for building, after which nothing happened until 1773 when they changed their minds and agreed to a plan by Atwood. At this Palmer put up an alternative suggestion with an offer by his senior partner, Thomas Jelly, to do the work for no more than a grant of 99-year leases on the houses and shops to be included in the design. It was rejected, which sparked off a furious controversy in the newspapers.

23 The Pump Room, from a print by J. C. Nattes, 1806

24 Pulteney Bridge, from a print of 1795

25 Pulteney Street and the Sydney Hotel (Holburne of Menstrie Museum)

26 Circus and Crescents (Lansdown Crescent top centre)

On 15 November, 15 years after the first proposals, seven after the foundation stone had been laid, Atwood fell through the floor of an old house in the market place and died. His young assistant, Thomas Baldwin, designed an elegant monument for the councillor's grave and in the following year was appointed City Surveyor at the age of 25. The slowly rising walls of Atwood's Guildhall were pulled down and new ones to Baldwin's design were commenced. This building, now extended by the wings Brydon added in 1891, showed a new spirit in the classical architecture of Georgian Bath, a spirit which Robert Adam was introducing into London, gayer, lighter, finer, more ornamented. A building, wrote Adam, should have a quality of 'movement', and even with its rusticated base it is this quality which Baldwin's Guildhall and its beautiful interior possesses. It is to be seen again in Baldwin's remodelling of the Baths area and, perhaps less successfully, in his Bathwick New Town, across the river.

The Bathwick estate had been sold by the Earl of Essex, Duke of Kingston, to the Pulteney family and the property had devolved on a Scottish member of the family, the wife of William Johnstone of Westerhall who assumed the arms and name of Pulteney and succeeded to the baronetcy on the death of his elder brother. Sir William having got an Act authorising a bridge to his estate, the Corporation in 1769 gave consent to its construction, and Pulteney employed his friend Robert Adam to make the design. It was finished in 1774, having ruined its builder, Reed. In 1805 it was found necessary to rebuild the western part. This delicate and charming bridge, formed as a street of little shops with end pavilions which were originally toll houses, has suffered a destruction of unity and scale, particularly on its north side, by the influence of commercial need – in other words they have stuck in great windows and hung a box on the back to increase floor space. Moreover it is choked with traffic. In spite of all this Pulteney Bridge still exerts great charm and the view of it over the river from the south is one of the delights of Bath.

Adam also produced plans for the layout of the estate but these were not adopted and instead the work was planned as a private venture by Baldwin, although the first building was actually a new prison in Grove Street designed externally as a Palladian mansion by Atwood, and part of a deal between Pulteney and the Corporation which gave him approach land to his bridge. The basement storey has since been exposed by the lowering of the Grove Street level. Baldwin started rather late, in 1788, with the octagonal Laura Place, named after Pulteney's daughter, and Pulteney Street, the longest, widest street in Bath, built on a platform over the flood plain of the river. The vista is closed by the Sydney Hotel (now Holburne of Menstrie Museum) designed by Harcourt Masters in 1796 to serve the pleasure gardens, or Vauxhall, behind. It was altered about 1920 by Sir Reginald Bloomfield, who removed an attic storey which had been added in 1836.

In 1791 the project for the gardens was approved by Miss Pulteney, shares were issued at £100 each, and Harcourt Masters appointed architect. They opened in May 1795 offering 'refreshments not only in quality, but also in quantity, equal, if not superior, to all other places of publick entertainment', 'Horns and Clarionets every Wednesday evening', and 'two Bowling Greens and two Swings'. Sunday swinging was not allowed. By September there had been added a Merlin Swing ('thought most conducive to health') and a Labyrinth which was 'so perplexing' that plans were sold at the entrance – 6d each. The hotel itself provided a ball room, tea rooms, and card rooms, a bandstand at the back, and a public-house, the Sydney Tap, in the basement. 'Tickets' were of metal and shareholders had very handsome silver ones. Sydney Gardens proved very popular until about 1840 when there was rapid decline. Sydenham, writing in 1905, cried Ichabod on the neglected gardens and ruinous hotel, but if one glory had departed another, quieter one, has taken its place thanks to the intervention of the Corporation.

Baldwin's plans were very grand but the optimistic show of squares and street in contemporary maps never materialised. The work came to an abrupt end in 1793 when failure of the Bath City Bank brought bankruptcy to Baldwin. He had already been sacked by the Corporation the year before after a mysterious row in some way connected with his management of the land and water revenues. He had been appointed Deputy Chamberlain as well as Surveyor and Inspector of the Baths in 1785 but in 1791 he was re-appointed solely as Architect and Surveyor and was ordered to hand over his account books. This he flatly refused to do and after a year of bickering he was removed from his post.

It is fortunate that before this happened he was to design and execute the new works in connection with the Bath Improvements Act of 1789, the Corporation's important, if belated, contribution to the Georgian townscape. As was normal with such schemes a special body of Improvement Commissioners was appointed to manage it. They were to be men of property, could not hold positions of profit under the Act, and had the power to appoint to any vacancies created in their ranks. Members included the Mayor, the Recorder, and worthies such as William Pulteney, Charles Meadows Pierrepont, and William Gore-Langton (later MP for Somerset) of nearby Newton Park. The main point of the Act was that it gave powers of compulsory purchase and authorised the taking of tolls on the roads into Bath. The scheme was financed by borrowing money on the security of these, which were farmed out, and the Commissioners were empowered to borrow up to £25,000. In addition the Corporation could contribute £7,163 16s 5d out of normal revenue, with a maximum of £700 in any one year.

Baldwin had already (1786 and 1788) flanked the old Pump Room with colonnades facing Stall Street. Behind the south colonnade he added a suite of private baths which were rebuilt with pride and doubtful taste by Davis in the 1880s, and are now (1972) being demolished to make way for a neo-Georgian block. For the Improvements he designed the present Pump Room (finished by Palmer) and linked it to his serpentine-fronted Cross Bath by the elegantly colonnaded, quadrant-ended Bath Street. Other new ways in the area (see map, p. 114) were Nash Street, Beau Street (formerly Bell Tree Lane), and Hot Bath Street. Union Street, designed by Baldwin but not constructed until 1802, was cut through the Bear Inn yard where previously, according to Smollet, 'the poor trembling valetudinarian is carried in a chair, betwixt the heels of a double row of horses, wincing under the curry-combs of grooms and postillions'.

The Bath Street area received later additions – a fountain by Pieroni (1859), a swimming Bath in Beau Street (1830, replaced 1922), reconstructed almshouses (St Catharine's, 1829; Bellot's, 1869), and the old United Hospital, now part of the Technical College. Designed by John Pinch, and erected in 1824–6 in a rather heavy Grecian style, it had considerable additions, including an attic storey, in about 1860 (Manners & Gill). The hospital was formed by amalgamating the city infirmary which had been in a large adjoining house, formerly tavern, and the casualty hospital, founded in 1789 in an old house on the north side of Kingsmead Square.

In Stall Street, the old White Hart, from which Eleazear Pickwick ran his coaches, was demolished in 1870 and replaced by the opulent Grand Pump Room Hotel (Wilson & Wilcox) with private baths behind (Davis, 1880). In 1960 the hotel was pulled down and replaced by the shops and flats of Arlington House, an innocuous piece of neo-Baldwinism.

The Improvements were part of the great building frenzy of the 1780s and early '90s, in which Baldwin's successor, John Palmer, and his early associate, John Eveleigh, played a notable part. Bath was continuing to move northward and, like the Woods, but in a lighter, wirier, less robust style, Palmer gave it a square and a crescent. St James's Square (1790–93) lacks complete cohesion, the proportions are not

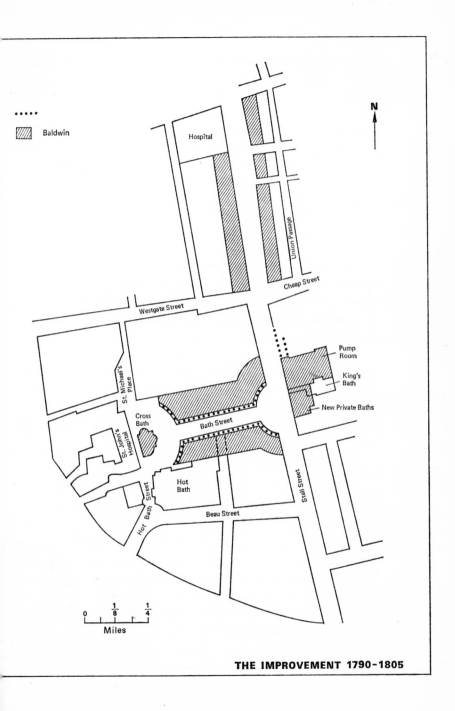

N

·····
▨ Baldwin

Hospital

Union Passage

Cheap Street

Westgate Street

Pump Room

King's Bath

New Private Baths

St. Michael's Place

Cross Bath

Bath Street

St. John's Hospital

Stall Street

Hot Bath

Hot Bath Street

Beau Street

0   ⅛   ¼
Miles

THE IMPROVEMENT 1790–1805

quite right and the angled exits break any sense of enclosure. Lansdown Crescent above (1789–93), with its serpentine double curves, is a hillside frill, less majestic and more human than the Royal Crescent. It achieves surprise by standing at the crest of a steep entry. To the west of it Eveleigh tucked in Somerset Place (1793) or at least the centre block of this little crescent. Here is a unique feature in Bath, a great segmental broken pediment decorated with swags and paterae, a satisfying surprise after all those triangles. The cluster of crescents is completed by Cavendish Crescent below by John Pinch, but this was a post-war addition of 1817–30.

Eveleigh had already (1788) designed Camden Crescent, with a rather bleak eastern aspect, sprung out on arches from the hillside so steep and treacherous that the supports at one end started to slide and the final section could not be completed, but his most ambitious project and the one which helped him into bankruptcy was a grandiose attempt to outshine Sydney Gardens, with pleasure grounds, hotel and houses out on the London Road. Under the foundations was buried an inscribed plate:

> The first Stone of Grosvenor House, Vauxhall, was laid on 24 June 1791, by John Eveleigh, Architect, being the Centre of 143 intended Houses, and at the entrance of Vauxhall Gardens, which will be built by Subscriptions, laid out with taste and elegance for the reception of Nobility, Gentry and the Public in general.

Eveleigh was a man of many parts – he offered to provide Nobility, Gentry, and Builders with marble or wood chimney pieces, copper ornaments, PATENT WATER CLOSETS ('without the least effluvia'), copper roofs, designs for Mansions, Villas, Dwellings either Gothick or Modern, and would undertake to superintend buildings, survey estates, or collect rents – but he was over-sanguine. Times were unsettled, public support failed, the City Bank crashed, and in November 1793 Eveleigh, along with Baldwin and others, was declared bankrupt. Unlike Baldwin, he never practised in Bath again, although he designed a new Guildhall for Plymouth – in the Gothic manner. The building at Grosvenor dragged on into the nineteenth century, the gardens were never completed, and the Hotel became for a time a College.

Palmer appears to have been more shrewd or more fortunate and was not involved in the crash, although he appears to have been briefly bankrupt in 1800. He was probably concerned in the two major developments by the river south-east of the city, at the close of this period. These were Green Park (1790–1808) and Norfolk Crescent (1795–1820). The former, standing starkly on its artificial platform which, according to Jane Austen, did not adequately defeat 'the damps', was completed during the Napoleonic Wars, but Norfolk Crescent long stood unfinished and had to wait for peacetime for completion. The wars certainly stemmed the flood of expansion, and there were contemporary comments on unfinished work, but building did not come to a complete halt. Relaxation, entertainment, medicine are precious things in time of war, and this in England was a professionals' war, which had little effect on society. It was not only at Brussels before Waterloo that there was 'sound of revelry by night', and it may be noted that 1804, the year when Napoleon massed his invasion barges at Boulogne, saw the laying of the foundation stone of the new Bath Theatre, and that the Retreat from Moscow in 1812 evoked a characteristic Bath response – a Charity Ball for Russian Aid.

Nevertheless, Bath was changing in social life and function. It was a gradual process and difficult to chart as much of the evidence comes from highly prejudiced writers; but there seems little doubt that by the end of the century Bath had become more respectable, duller, more snobbish, more middle-class, and more of a service and residential centre than in the high days of Beau Nash. Subsequent Masters of Ceremonies were lightweight figures, private entertaining had gained pre-eminence over public assembly, the lists of visitors contained fewer prestigious names, the Corporation failed to entice George III from the rival delights of Cheltenham, the number of lodging houses decreased, the number of shops multiplied, and the rate books show an increasing amount of permanent residence. The city which had taught manners to the capital was now considered rather old-fashioned, somewhat strait-laced even (in spite of the brothels in Avon Street), a bit of a bore – but fortunately not too expensive, and well-provided with food. It certainly appealed to Fanny Burney who wrote in 1816 that it was 'in England, the only place for us, since here, all the year round, there is always the town at command, and always the country for prospect, exercise and delight'. According to Hannah More wartime Bath was 'never so gay', where 'princes and kings that will be, and princes and kings that have been, pop upon you at every corner' (1797), so perhaps the glamour of Bath was not as faded as some writers would suggest.

It had been a marvellous century. Not only had a new, unique, city been created, a modern delight and planner's nightmare, but the roll of visitors reads like an eighteenth-century *Who's Who*, from Arblay, Madam d' (see Burney F.) to York, Frederick Augustus, Duke of. Here is Sarah Churchill putting up with Bath as long as the waters do the Duke some good; Pope popping into the town at regular intervals; the elder Pitt, MP for the city, with a house in the Circus; the younger Pitt hearing of the Prussian defeat at Austerlitz while he is visiting at Shockerwick House; Nelson recovering from the fevers of the West Indian station and thinking Bath 'Bermuda to the rest of England'; Dr Johnson visiting Mrs Thrale before she lost his esteem by becoming Mrs Piozzi; Mrs Piozzi becoming bluestocking Queen of Bath but finding the bottom of the town a stewpot and the top a griddle (Pope had called Lower Bath 'a sulphurous pit'); Gainsborough gradually raising his prices from five to 100 guineas during his 16 years in Bath before he

27 Ralph Allen. From a portrait of 1754

28 Prior Park and the Palladian bridge. From a watercolour of c.1770

quarrelled with waspish Thicknesse and left for London; Clive living 'in a little pomp' in Westgate Buildings; Coleridge preaching in a blue coat and white waistcoat to a thin congregation at the Unitarian chapel in Trim Street; the young Southey staying with his aunt; the four-year-old Walter Scott seeing his first play, *As You Like It*, at the Theatre Royal in 1775; Wesley confounding Beau Nash; Horace Walpole hating his three months in 1766 and showing equal detestation of the hills, the houses, and Lord Chesterfield; Herschel playing the organ in the Octagon, conducting the orchestra in the Assembly Rooms, taking music pupils, and finding time, with the help of his remarkable sister, to manufacture monster telescopes, chart the heavens, and discover a new planet which was first named Georgium Sidus, and then Uranus; Fielding working on *Tom Jones* at Twerton and dining at Prior Park; Christopher Anstey writing the enormously successful *New Bath Guide*, a lively account in verse of a family visit to Bath, which Gibbon carefully explained to the French was an excellent example of 'what the English call Humour'; all this, and so much more, needs a separate book, a big, fat book with footnotes, a book which was written by a Frenchman, Barbeau, in 1904. He called it *Life and Letters at Bath in the Eighteenth Century* and it is unfortunately out of print. There is not room to rewrite it here.

No general account of eighteenth-century Bath would, however, be complete without a mention of the local millionaire – well, near-millionaire. Ralph Allen was born in 1693 in Cornwall, the son of an innkeeper. Pope called him 'low born' but later changed this to 'humble', explaining that he had meant no derogation. After some experience in Exeter he came to Bath in 1710 as assistant to the postmistress, Mary Collins, whose office was in the remains of St Michael's *intra muros*, and in March 1712 he took over from her at a salary of £25 per annum. Three years later, when Queen Anne had been succeeded by George of Hanover, the Jacobites rose, and Major-General George

Wade descended with horse and foot on Bath, a city suspected to contain a strong anti-Hanoverian faction. The result was a spectacular haul of 200 horses, 11 chests of firearms, a hogshead of swords, another of cartridges, and three cannons, and a mortar, the discovery of which is attributed, is some way not known, to information from Allen. Certainly he made a firm friend in Wade who gave financial backing to his application to take over the cross-posts in the west and the by-way post (i.e. letters between stages on the main post routes) for England and South Wales. Allen did not invent the system of cross-posting but by administrative ability he made it for the first time extremely profitable so that he was not only able to pay the Post Office something like £6,000 a year for the privilege of administering them but was able to make a very handsome, if concealed, profit for himself. How he did it was, he maintained, nobody's business but his own.

His concern was communication, and in 1724 he became a stockholder and one of the three treasurers in the Avon Navigation, apparently being the main influence in the building of a new road bridge over the Avon which is still called Newbridge although structurally now the oldest, even with its early nineteenth-century remodelling. In 1725 he was elected a freeman and councillor, but in the council records his name is notable for absence (he was Mayor for only one year, in 1742), and his civic influence has been exaggerated, principally on the basis of a cartoon 'The Knights of Bathe, or the One Headed Corporation', issued in 1763 the year before he died. This referred to a particular political incident. Through Allen's influence the Elder Pitt had in 1757 become MP for Bath. In 1763 Pitt's enemies, the King's men, concluded the Peace of Paris which ended the Seven Years' War, and the MP for Bath was incensed to receive from the Corporation an address to be forwarded to George III congratulating him on so 'adequate' a peace, a peace which Pitt had publicly anathematised as 'inadequate'. Allen was known as a man of influence, one to whom the

local dignitaries turned for advice, and he took responsibility for drafting the resolution which was different from
the original proposed by the Corporation; it is not surprising
that a pro-Pitt cartoon should show the Corporation as
faceless sycophants of the great man.

Pitt was furious with his electors and with heavy irony
confessed himself to Allen as 'but ill qualified to form pre-
tensions to the future favour of gentlemen who are come to
think so differently from me on matters of the highest
importance to the national welfare'. However, he continued
to represent them for another three years, and never lost his
personal regard for Allen, 'a truly good man' whose friendship he regarded as amongst his 'happiest advantages and
first honours'. This was no conventional rhetoric; every
account we have of Allen, the Squire Allworthy of *Tom
Jones*, shows him as a man with a gift for friendship –
simple, unassuming, considerate, generous, yet with a
quality of mind and character which commanded respect.
The only sour note was sounded by the cantankerous
Thicknesse who regarded the simplicity as an unsuccessful
attempt to conceal 'a Man deeply charged with Pride', but
Thicknesse was unreliable and a great hater, arranging for
his gravestone to read 'Governor of Landguard Fort and
unfortunately father to Lord Audley' and ordering that on
his death his hand should be cut off and sent to his son.
When Pope left Allen £150 in his will, 'being, to the best
of my calculations, the account of what I have received from
him', Allen's only remark on this insulting gesture was that
'Mr Pope was always a bad accomptant, and if, to the £150
he had put a cipher more, he had come nearer the truth' and
he donated the sum to the Bath Hospital, the venture which
had brought together Allen, Wood, Nash, and Dr Oliver,
and for the building of which he had given £1,000 and the
stone from his quarries.

It was by the development of these that Allen left his
permanent mark on Bath in a uniformity of splendid stone.
In 1726 he began to acquire and develop the quarries in

Combe Down, high above the south side of the city, and soon afterwards engaged a Bristol engineer, John Pudmore, to build a railway down what is now Ralph Allen Drive to carry the huge blocks of stone weighing 4–6 tons. The timber rails were 3 ft 9 in apart (approx. 1.14 m.), carrying flat oak wagons with cast-iron wheels. Horses pulled the empty wagons back uphill. At Dolemead Allen established a wharf with a special crane which, according to Wood in 1735, was 'allowed by the Curious to be a Masterpiece'. The railway, which was one of the wonders of the age, lowered stone prices from 10s to 7s 6d a ton at Dolemeads, and was an enormous success. Soon after Allen's death, however, the cranes were sold and the railway dismantled, possibly because road improvements had made it redundant. It had helped to make Allen his second fortune.

His great mansion, Prior Park, where he entertained Pope and his wife refused to entertain Pope's friend Martha Blount, where he kept open house to Fielding and Pitt (who entered two horses in the races on Claverton Down), and gave a home to Warburton, his son-in-law, was built partly as an advertisement for the Bath stone which was not then held in high regard. The architect was the elder Wood who had already (1727) designed a richly Corinthian extension to Allen's town house, but the building was finished by the Clerk to the Works, Richard Jones (*c.* 1703–73) owing to some temporary disagreement, and it was Jones who built the Palladian bridge in the gardens (1750) to the same design as at Wilton (1736), hauling the stone by what may have been the first self-acting inclined plane in Britain.

After Warburton, who had, by Allen's influence, become Bishop of Gloucester in 1759, moved to the Palace ten years later, the house passed through various hands before it was acquired by John Thomas, a Quaker, who supervised the construction of the Kennet and Avon Canal. Then in 1830 Prior Park was bought by Bishop Baines and turned into a Catholic seminary, after which it became the boys' boarding school which it is today. In 1836 was added the impressive sweep of the outer stairway, designed by Goodridge, but also in this year was a disastrous fire and although, fortunately, Wood's chapel was not affected most of the interior was rebuilt in a somewhat tasteless style. In 1863 was completed a large and impressive church at the western end. Although this throws the composition out of scale, Prior Park with its great centre block jutting into a hexastyle (six columned) porch, its sweeping wings, its curving, balustraded staircase, and its little bridge in the grounds, remains one of the most impressive sights of eighteenth-century Bath – 'the most ambitious and the most complete re-creation of Palladio's villas on English soil' (Pevsner).

8 *Steam, Squalor, and Civic Pride*

The Nineteenth Century

Eighteenth-century Bath had been a carousel with a fountain in the middle, revolving to the sound of bells and bands, crowded with an ever-changing throng of the famous, would-be-famous, and would-know-famous, hopping on and off, quarrelling, laughing, intriguing, sweating, complaining, exclaiming, propping up gouty legs, stealing illicit kisses, and in general creating so much glitter and brouhaha that when the merry-go-round ran down and the fairground was deserted life itself seemed to have left the place. This was very far from the truth.

The spirit of the new century was less frenetic, less superficially attractive, more earnest and therefore duller, but its achievements were considerable and lasting. The administrative area of the city was trebled, the population nearly doubled, and the masters of the expanded city were no longer a self-perpetuating oligarchy but, after 1835, a body elected by the citizens. They doubled the size of the old hospital and built a new one, added a large concert hall to the old Pump Room, created parks, an art gallery, a swimming bath, gave the town a new water supply, promoted gas lighting and then electricity, resurfaced the streets, and trebled the size of the Guildhall in order to cope with the new responsibilities of local government. They dealt more efficiently than many places with the cholera epidemic of

1832. They revealed and exhibited the long-forgotten Roman baths. A lively social conscience, public and private, multiplied the charities in the city and placed the old ones on a sounder footing. There was a great increase in educational facilities.

Shops proliferated, there was a small but significant industrial development, building went on apace from spacious Italianate or neo-Gothic villas through acres of decent by-law housing to the less admirable working-class streets. There was a flurry of church building for the new areas, and a renovation of the Abbey. By the end of the century nearly every important corner site in the shopping spine had been knocked down and rebuilt with ostentation and out of scale. So energetic, indeed, had been the Victorian efforts to bring the city into the modern age that some citizens felt the need in 1909 to found the 'Old Bath Preservation Society', for the nineteenth century had to grapple with problems still with us and stronger yet, of reconciling the excellencies of the past with the needs of the present – and having propounded a solution, if solution there is, finding a way to pay for it. Which leads us to a fundamental question of economy.

Bath had a rough time financially through most of the nineteenth century. Her economic base was very narrow and consisted mostly of service trades and industries, from shop-keeping to cabinet and carriage making; dependent on free-spending visitors there was little else which could create prosperity. Her gradual change from resort to residence could only have resulted in a growth of wealth if the people who came to live there had an outside source of income to support the physicians, domestic servants, milliners, shoe-makers, builders, labourers, and traders who formed the bulk of the working population, and this was true of only a limited number. The economic imbalance has been well illustrated by Neale (*Economic conditions and the working class movement in Bath 1800–1840*, ts of MA *thesis*, 1963, Bath library) and was mentioned by Egan in his *Walks through*

Bath (1819) but, although the latter hoped for some increase in manufacturing with proposed improvement of communications from Bristol, the picture he gives of Bath is one of prosperity and optimism. He is careful to skirt round the declining areas, however, apart from Avon Street (now vanished) 'the receptacle for unfortunate women', which he exhibits with a kind of fascinated horror, although his picture does not accord well with a newspaper comment of the following year that Bath 'from having been one of the gayest, most frequented, and most desirable places of fashionable resort, is now fast falling into neglect, and is surrounded by all the symptoms of premature decay'. Yet 1819 saw the streets of Bath shining in the new gas lighting, and 1820 the consecrating of the fine new Gothic church of St Mary's, Bathwick.

In the year 1840 when the GWR came to Bath and work started on a whole new group of streets between the station and the town, 'Lud Hudibras' wrote in his pamphlet on *The Present Decline*: 'empty streets, deserted shops, tradesmen without customers, goods lacking buyers, the few amusements we have left desert', you could, he said, have fired a cannon right up Milsom Street without hitting anyone, except perhaps a shopkeeper who had come out to contemplate 'the gloomy void'. He was quite sure he knew the causes, which were psychological – the 'besotted pride' of the tradespeople (which stopped them cooperating) and narrow-minded bigotry of the clergy (which frightened people off the amusements). Again, in 1867, when the city had just got a new Sewage Bill, we hear of *The Wants of Bath*.

What is remarkable is that as Bath staggered from year to year with no lack of doom-laden prophets of collapse it continued to build, modify, and expand. There was always something going on. If 1819 was the Year of the Gas, 1851 was the Year of the Water, 1866 the Year of the Sewage, and 1880 the Tramway Year. If 1805 saw the opening of the new theatre, 1825 saw the founding of the

Literary Society, 1830 the opening of Victoria Park, 1859 the new YMCA building, and 1897 the Concert Hall extension to the Pump Room. It would be convenient if development could be shown to relate to periods which start with a major event such as the opening of the Kennet and Avon Canal (1810), the end of the Napoleonic Wars (1815), the Municipal reform (1835), or the discovery of the Roman Baths (1880), but this would be historically untrue, and the nearest we can reasonably get to a pattern is to say that the first half of the century was one of considerable economic difficulty which saw the founding of many charity organisations, the third quarter saw a slight recovery, and the last quarter was a time of reviving activity, with the town for a time recovering its importance as a spa as well as developing a certain amount of new industry. This final time can be considered as a whole but for the rest it is more appropriate to select certain themes for treatment than to attempt a chronological canter over the whole field. These themes are transport, services, government, and building.

The previous century had started with the Avon navigation which linked Bath and Bristol, the new one commenced with the extension of water communications to London with the opening of the Kennet and Avon canal on 9 November 1810, with a barge laden with 40 tons of stone leaving, and barges with over 800 sacks of flour from Newbury coming in. The authorising Act had been passed in 1794 but the canal was a long time building, partly because of rising costs which produced a number of crises and necessitated three supplementary Acts to enable more money to be raised, and partly because the committee, against the advice of their eminent engineer, John Rennie, insisted on Bath stone for the locks. Much of this stone was neither of the best quality nor laid with understanding, so that it had to be replaced. Diligent search in a path from the Warminster road to Bathampton Down reveals the stone blocks on which were fastened the rails which carried stone down to the canal building.

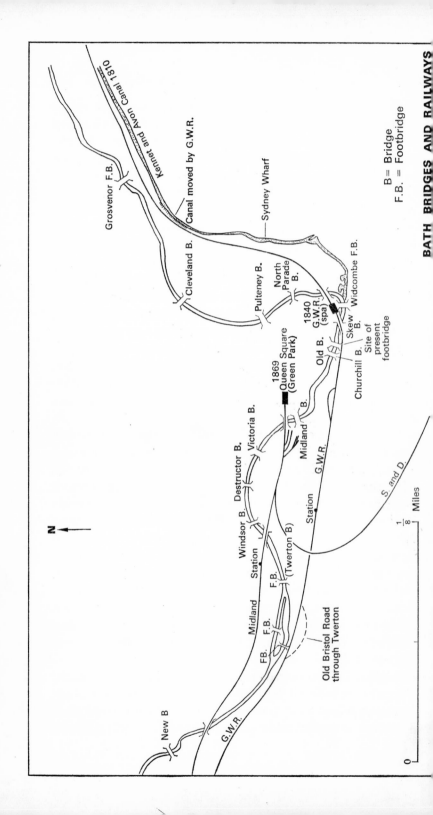

BATH BRIDGES AND RAILWAYS

B = Bridge
F.B. = Footbridge

Grosvenor F.B.

Kennet and Avon Canal 1810

Canal moved by G.W.R.

Sydney Wharf

Cleveland B.

Pulteney B.

North Parade B.

Widcombe F.B.

1840 G.W.R. (spa)

Skew B.

Churchill B. Site of present footbridge

Old B.

1869 Queen Square (Green Park)

Midland B.

Victoria B.

Destructor B.

Windsor B.

G.W.R.

S. and D.

Station

Station

Midland

F.B.

F.B.

(Twerton B.)

F.B.

Old Bristol Road through Twerton

New B

G.W.R.

N

0   1/8   Miles

Following the Avon along the Limpley Stoke valley, where it twice crosses the river by the Avoncliff and Dundas aqueducts, the canal curves round the hills south of Bath, cuts through Sydney Gardens where it is spanned by iron bridges from the local firm of Stothert's, and passes under Cleveland House, one-time Bath headquarters of the K & A company. In the floor of the house is a trap-door through which tradition says, maybe with truth, messages were exchanged with barges passing beneath. The final stage drops down to the river by a flight of seven locks with attendant reservoirs. At the top was a pumping station (they were not allowed to use the domestic supply springs of the parish) whose Classical chimney can still be seen.

In 1811 there were proposals to carry the canal on to Bristol. The Avon navigation, which the K & A acquired, was not doing very well ('no bustle at the quay', said Egan), and the wharfs of the two waterways were separated by the Old Bridge. The Bill aroused furious controversy – one gentleman argued, for instance, that access to new markets would enable the Somerset coalfields to raise their prices, another that the destruction of property entailed was too great, while the Corporation refused to support the scheme unless costly flood-prevention measures were incorporated – and why, said some, abandon a navigation which, with a smaller investment, could be made adequate? The scheme never came into being.

The K & A was a successful venture, but in 1835 the committee were in a state of alarm, for a Railway Bill for the Great Western was before Parliament. At first they spent a great deal of money on fighting it but eventually settled for a compensation of £10,000 and in 1839, when they were carrying construction materials for the rival line, they enjoyed a peak revenue of £52,347. But their alarm was justified; by 1842 receipts had dropped to just over £32,000, not due to lack of freight but to a ruinous price-war with their rival. So, on the principle that 'If you can't beat 'em, join 'em', they sponsored a Bill in 1845 for the

London, Newbury and Bath Direct Railway along the line of
the canal. It was rejected, and in 1852 they sold out to the
GWR. Then followed a rapid and serious decline, although
timber was still carried from Bristol to the Vale of Pewsey
as late as 1929.

With nationalisation in 1947 the canal passed to the BTC
(British Transport Commission) who in 1955 applied to
Parliament for its abandonment but was told that the canal
should not be allowed to deteriorate beyond its state at the
time – which was generally bad. Since then two things have
happened. Firstly there is now a greater sensitivity to
environmental quality and a greater appreciation of the
importance of adequate and varied provision for leisure-
time activities. Secondly the canal has been blessed since
1951 with the untiring and practical devotion of the Kennet
and Avon Association which in June 1961 turned itself into
a Trust and by publicity, petition, and restoration fieldwork
has kept the canal issue, and the canal itself, alive. In Bath
its most notable activity has been, with financial assistance
from the Corporation, the rescue and renovation of the
Widcombe locks. This urban waterway has great amenity
potential and it is to be hoped the practical concern of private
people will be further supported by government action at
both local and national levels.

While the canal was being cut the roads were deteriorat-
ing. Seeking help, the Bath Turnpike Trust turned to the
nationally famous expert, James Loudon MacAdam and
on 25 March 1826 appointed him General Surveyor of the
Bath roads at a salary of £600 per annum, with his son
William as assistant. The annual cost of 'sustaining' the
roads was not to exceed £7,000. At the time of his appointment for a five-year period the Trust was in financial
difficulties. Although they had previously been able to earn
from £12,000 to £14,000 per annum and in the previous year
had an income of £10,611 they had not been able to pay a
dividend for four years and the debt on the last year stood
at £28,279.

MacAdam's appointment was not made without opposition and several 'experienced Commissioners' did not believe that he could make the roads pay at the sum agreed and that they would, in fact, deteriorate. It was therefore decided that after a five-year trial a sub-Committee should investigate and report. In preparation for this the roads were 'pitted', that is trial bores were made, for comparison with pitting done at the end of the period.

On 4 June 1831 the Committee on the State of the Roads, the Expenditure and Future Management reported that MacAdam had done the work with £286 to spare and with the acquisition of £604 of capital equipment in the form of 10 horses, 12 carts, and harness, and that new pitting showed that the roads had improved, the depth of material being greater. They therefore proposed that the Surveyor and his son should be retained but that their salaries should be cut by £100 and less money – £6,300 – allowed for future work. This sounds ungrateful but it was accepted by MacAdam, and was based on the argument that the major reconstruction had been finished so that the Surveyor's work would become less onerous and would be mainly carried out by his son, who could not expect such a high salary.

The report also noted other improvements. The roads were properly supplied with direction posts and milestones showing boundaries and names of parishes (some of these cast-iron signs still exist); 'Mr M'Adam' had introduced a rigid and systematic examination of accounts; arrears had been paid off; there had been avoidance or cutting down of hills at Kingsdown (Box), Dunkerton, Newbridge, and Marksbury, and improvements at or near the bridge over the Avon which 'had so long held pre-eminence among Road Nuisances'.

The major works followed Parliamentary approval given in the Bath Act of 1829 and in Bath resulted in the lengthening and widening of Newbridge, the cutting of Newbridge road 'past the lime-kilns' and the moving of Newton Turn-

pike (see map, p. 142). This was finished in 1835 at a final
cost of £5,777 6s 8d, about 25 per cent more than the
original estimates, a situation not unknown today. Business
picked up for a while but in 1836 the Commissioners were
worried about coming railway competition. They estimated
they would lose £889 a year in Bath–Bristol coach trade and
£822 from Bath–London, but they were even more concerned about the prospect of losing the coal carriage from
Farmborough to the south and determined to concentrate
their dwindling resources on this road. In 1851 the Corporation took over responsibility for the roads in the city and
eventually the tolls were extinguished.

Tolls continued, however, on the new bridges which were
put over the Avon, the chief being the cast-iron, single-span,
Cleveland Bridge (Goodridge, 1827) and the North Parade
Bridge (Tierney Clark, 1835), also iron but with stone
abutments. These encouraged growth east of the river, but
Bath was also spreading west and here Mr Dredge put in
his patent Victoria Suspension Bridge (1836) at a cost of
£1,650. He did a good deal of publicity for his idea, holding
trials with models of different constructions and enlisting the
enthusiastic aid of Lord Western. He wrote to the Prime
Minister, Melbourne, advocating that Dredge should be
allowed to put his proposals for rebuilding the Menai
Bridge, which he was prepared to do for only the sale of the
old ironwork, and questioning the monopoly of Brunel and
Telford in the field. 'Why,' wrote Western, 'if he can build
the proposed Clifton Bridge as he says he could for one-third
less than Mr Brunel's estimate, is he not called upon to do
so?' He was not called, and his bridge remains an interesting
monument to an idea that never caught on. 'It is neither',
wrote the Deputy Engineer in 1926, 'a good example of
type or design . . . and will probably be demolished.' It is
still there (1972).

Railway development also encouraged cross-river links.
In 1863 the Widcombe footbridge was built at the back of
the GWR station and was the scene of a disaster in 1877.

The Bath and West (founded in 1775) was holding its
annual show on Beechen Cliff and the GWR advertised
Widcombe bridge as the quickest way by foot from the
station. All might have been well if tolls had been taken at
the railway end but they were taken on the other side and
some 200–300 people were crowded on the bridge when it
fractured and flung them to the river 26 feet below. Eight
were killed and the proprietors were successfully prosecuted
for manslaughter. The bridge was rebuilt and still stands.
In 1869 the Midland railway had reached Bath so there
were two lines running parallel on opposite sides of the river.
To link Twerton and Weston stations the Bath and Weston
Bridge Company was formed in 1893 and built a bridge to
serve a neighbourhood which it said was 'rapidly increasing
(with) hundreds of houses in the course of erection'.

Like the Kennet and Avon, the Great Western had
problems in getting through hill-girt Bath and they met
them with a succession of cuttings, embankments, tunnels,
and bridges, notably the skew-bridge over the Avon, constructed first in wood and then replaced with stone and iron.
In August 1840 over 1,000 men were working by day and
by the lurid light of huge fires by night, and even, as the
reporter was pained to note, on the Sabbath, to get the works
at Bath complete. The race against time was won and on a
sunny Monday, on the last day of August, thousands of
people assembled on the hill slopes above to see the first
train, the sunlight gleaming on the copper dome of the
engine, roll in on the broad gauge (7-foot) line, just over
half an hour after leaving Bristol, to the sound of 'merry
peals' from the Abbey (the K & A had started with gunfire
on Sydney wharf). Greeted by station staff in their green
uniforms, the directors then went to the White Lion in the
High Street for 'a splendid breakfast'. Throughout the day
people were crowding on to the carriages for the novelty of
the ride 'with none of the bumpiness', it was proudly
reported, 'of some other lines'. It was calculated that some
720 first-class and some 1,200 second-class passengers

travelled that day, pulled by Fireball, Lynx, Meridian, or Arrow (built by Stothert and Slaughter at Bristol; the others had come from Lancashire and Newcastle). They would have to wait a year before they could get through to London; and Mr Pickwick and other coach proprietors were quick to announce services to Farington station where they could pick up a London train, as well as offering, as did Edward Mitchell of the Sawclose, 'carriage per GWR' to Bristol. Pickwick also organised a town horse omnibus service at 6d a trip to meet every train, the round trip starting and ending at his White Hart Inn.

The economic consequences of the rail link must not be exaggerated. There was no rapid expansion of industry and the working population continued to depend in the main, and with consequent distress, on service activities; indeed the railway system as a whole tended to detract from Bath's position, focusing activities, both for pleasure and industry, on other places. The physical results, however, were considerable and lasting.

There was, for instance, the station itself, with its four tracks, the centre ones used for parking trains, spanned by a great roof (since removed) with iron pillars inconveniently near the edge of the platforms, with its carriage approaches on both fronts (now only one), and its row of arches carrying the railway to the west. Here was the modern miracle, steam locomotion, come to Bath at a time when it was possible to build in glass and iron, but come to a city whose architecture was firmly fixed in the Classical mode. What design, what style should be used? In the event, Brunel chose a neo-Tudor façade and crenellated his bridge as if engine drivers were expected to engage in bow and arrow battles with the hostile natives.

If we stand with our back to the station we shall be looking up Manvers Street to the edge of Georgian Bath in Pierrepont Street and the Parades; to our left is Dorchester Street leading to the Old Bridge (the site of the presnte footbridge). Both these streets were built by the GWR over what was then open land, although maps had shown hopeful development plans in dotted lines. Actually, half of Dorchester Street was already there, it was simply a case of continuing it from the Steam Flour Mills to the station; but the other had to be completely new and was to be kept in repair by the GWR until two-thirds of it had been lined with buildings when the responsibility would devolve on the landowner, Lord Manvers. This is possibly why it took a long time to complete the building programme, which produced on the west side a High Victorian row of only modest ostentation; a war-time bomb behind them left a space for the present harmless and necessary bus station. At the station end are two rather fine, curving-cornered buildings, large and late (1901), originally hotels. The fierceness of the arguments over whether they should be destroyed or preserved illustrates how rapidly the cycles of taste are turning. Perhaps it will not be long before Bathonians are venerating instead of anathematising their Empire Hotel. After all, we are beginning to look with admiration and affection on the cinema buildings of the thirties and our children are buying expensive versions of the fashions their parents discarded as out of date. In this new Victorian age of technical advance, disgust with the social results, uncertainty of the future, nostalgia for the past, and interest in drugs and odd philosophies, perhaps even the undistinguished buildings of the present will become objects of affection and even approval in a generation or two.

Two further changes of 1840 may be noted. To get out on the east the railway had to nudge the canal to one side, shoring it up with an impressive masonry cliff by Hampton Row, while to get in on the west the embankment cut off Twerton High Street which was a section of the turnpike road to Bristol. Here the GWR had to provide a new length of road on the north side and connect it to the village through arches. This was near where the Avon Navigation had previously straightened their route by the Weston Cut (the adjacent Dolphin Inn now has its face turned to the road, originally it was entered from the canal side), creating an island of textile mills until the death of the industry and the recent flood-prevention activities altered the map.

The Midland railway had a rather easier approach line when it broke its 'no-poaching' agreement and on 4 August 1869 linked through from Mangotsfield to a fine Classical-fronted station which was then called Queen Square but was renamed Green Park with more geographical truth on nationalisation. There was no official opening ceremony and, when Mr Stone decorated his Porter Stores with flags and a scroll 'Success to the Midland Railway', no one followed his example. Nevertheless hundreds of people came, most to catch the 7.40 for the penny trip to the nearest station and arrive back seventeen minutes later on the next train in from Bristol.

The line was closed in 1966* and the consequent dereliction of this large, imposing building has been a sad thing. In 1874 the Somerset and Dorset joined it from the south in a state of financial exhaustion after its mile-long tunnel under Combe Down and in the following year sold out, allowing the Midland to poke a long tentacle down and latch on to the Southern system, so that Green Park has meant to so many people the start of seaside holidays and excursion trips. Part of the abandoned line, which effectively cut off the building development of South Twerton and Lower Oldfield Park in the 1880s, may become a linear park.

Within the town sedan chairs were being replaced by the wheeled Bath chairs. In general the chair stands were in the higher income northern areas, the hackney stands in a circle round the central shopping region which remained a feature of the place up to the Second World War, but in common with other towns hackney carriage stands became a feature of Bath. There was also a great increase of light carriages, 'flies', for private hire – the Directory of 1900 lists 62 fly

* In July 1972 it was bought by the Corporation, price and purpose undisclosed.

proprietors while the 1850 publication does not even
mention them. There were also about a dozen livery stables.
We have seen that a horse omnibus service started to link
with the railway but another advance in public transport
came in 1880 when Bath Tramways began a service on a
4-foot gauge line for one and three-quarter miles from the
station through the town out to the Grosvenor on the
London Road. It had seven one-horse cars, with an extra
horse on the steeper slopes, and it was not a success. In 1884
it sold out to the Patent Cable Tramways Company (although they never used cables in Bath) who went bankrupt
four years later. Meanwhile the Bath Omnibus company
had been formed and they bought the tramway, changing
their name to Bath Road Car and Tramways Ltd. They were
only a little more successful, having bad luck with blizzards
and pink-eye (in the horses) and in 1902 were happy to sell
the line to a new company, Bath Electric Tramways who
changed *their* name to the Bath Carriage and Omnibus Co.
Ltd. The Corporation had already (1900) applied for a
Light Railway Order which would provide for an extensive
network. In 1903 the system was ready and Board of Trade
inspectors were waiting at the Guildhall for their tour by
tram. Unfortunately there was a fault at the power station
in Walcot Street and they had to do the first part by carriage.
However, the inspectors finished electrically and the next
year the system started a regular service which was to
continue until 1939 when the buses took over completely,
the lines were ripped up, and the cars sent to their death,
mourned by many.

Theories of urban development tend to lean heavily on
the transport factor but there is no such clear relationship
in Bath. One reason is that such theories tend to under-
estimate both the distances people of all classes were prepared to walk and the importance of the working-man's
horse, the bicycle (by 1900 there were 22 Cycle Agents in
Bath – today there are six listed in the Yellow Pages, but
there are 23 car distributors). More locally relevant are the

related facts that Bath never developed a large element of industry nor spread excessively far. Industry was on a small scale neither requiring to bring together large numbers of people nor large quantities of bulky materials; moreover it produced for a local market and was therefore less influenced by large-scale transport requirements and much more by site availability. The nineteenth-century spread of Bath is much more reasonably understood in terms of topography than of transport. External communications came, as in Roman times, more from the location of Bath than from its attraction, and internal communications were developed to serve areas which had already come into existence; indeed this was the contemporary argument for their initiation.

Whereas a great deal of Georgian building in Bath must be thought of in terms of accommodation for visitors, nineteenth-century development was more for permanent residence and in particular for the middle class which was growing in numbers and affluence. (Incidentally, a change in provision for visitors is shown by the directories: in 1850 they list over 200 lodging house keepers and no hotels – inns are noted – and in 1900 no lodging house keepers are mentioned but there are 28 hotels. Lodging houses were referred to in the Health of Towns Report but there were doss-houses of which one in Abbey Green was 'a model' and one in Avon Street was 'a disgrace to the city'.) The influx of residents was very much a phenomenon of the post-war, pre-railway era – the three central parishes, St James, Sts Peter and Paul, and St Michael increased by 16 per cent from 1801 to 1811, by 21 per cent in the next ten years, but only two per cent from 1841 to '51. The later spread, at a lower housing density apart from the poorer quarters, was more due to migration outwards. The Victorians had become Romantic, they had turned away from the public life of the Georgians towards private entertainment and the family; the ideal was now the suburban villa, towns were places to escape from if possible, and the more money you made the further out you got until England was littered with a new breed of squires who supported their land on the profits of industry and commerce. It was the age of the snob, whose ambition was to leap the social gulf between 'trade' and the landed classes. If a man couldn't do it himself, he might be able to send his son to a public school (greatly to the school's financial benefit), marry him into the coveted class and leave enough money for him to be able to ignore his origin. Like all generalisation this is both true and false but it is not too fanciful to see in the semi-detached neo-Gothic or neo-Classical villa with its patch of garden, its laurel hedges, and its tiny conservatory, a miniaturised version of a great estate. So began a movement which continued through in the building 'estates' of the twentieth century and which in the nineteenth, particularly the last quarter, lined the hill roads to north and south with a new house-and-garden form which was in some ways a reversion to the early medieval city without its virtue of compactness.

The idea that 'the Englishman's home is his castle' implies insulation and isolation. Many people could not, of course, afford this, and so the miniaturised castles had to be tacked together to form rows—the Victorian terrace. At best, and particularly after the regulations which stemmed from the 1875 Health Act, this produced some very substantial housing as well as smaller, decent habitations which authorities have only just come to realise as worth modernisation rather than replacement. In some of the Bath terraces the classical tradition with a flat front and parapeted roof continues, but more usually we find bay windows and gables. Bath stone is not everywhere in evidence – in some areas we find the grey Pennant, a coal-measure sandstone, and in a few cases red brick – and it was not until 1925 that the Corporation obtained a local Act which ensured that new building would be in Bath stone or an artificial facsimile, a move which anticipated national planning legislation by 20 years. Stone surfaces are, of course, often facings – in Georgian buildings they tend to hide rubble walls, in the later building they are hiding brick and in our own period are concealing breeze blocks. A major change that took place in building materials in the nineteenth century with the coming of rail transport was the substitution of Welsh slate for stone tiles on the roofs.

Some terraces were mean and poor, often with walls of a single thickness of six-inch ashlar, with one room up and one down and a shared privy out at the back. Particularly nasty was 'the filthy, odious Dolemeads' which sprang up at the terminus of the Kennet and Avon canal and whose 'very poor description of houses' were awash whenever the river rose. It has however a substantial Ebenezer chapel (1820) nearby and a sound schoolroom 'for the labouring classes' opened by the Bishop in 1856.* After 1804 there was also a gasometer. It is not surprising that this was the first area to be dealt with under the powers conferred by the Housing of the Working Classes Act of 1890. The scheme was proposed in 1896, approved by the Local Government Board in 1899 with permission to borrow £10,500, and started in 1900 when Mr Toogood's tender was accepted. Property was demolished, the ground level raised thirteen feet, concrete for roads and foundations put in, and terraces of red brick houses sprang up to be let at five shillings a week. The Medical Officer of Health hoped that they would continue to be the homes of the poorer people.

West of Dolemeads, after a break, was the Holloway area with an unsavoury reputation, being noted for its thieves, beggars, 'dreary pot-houses', 'dingy chandler's stores', and the ill-used horses of the coal carrying trade. It was a 'rookery' which made an uncomfortable beat for the one constable, conspicuous in his white trousers, swallow-tail coat, and top hat with a bit of oilcloth on the top. The area persisted, in increasing decrepitude, until recent years when it has been swept away, along with some small but not

---

* The present school was opened in 1900, again by a Bishop. It was 'Jacobean' and the floor raised seven feet above the playground to beat the floods.

unpleasant terraces, leaving the chunky neo-Perpendicular
church of St Mark (Manners, 1830) which, set against
Beechen Cliff (bought by the Corporation for £150 in
1860), is still a landmark for railway travellers.

On the north of the river, stinking with untreated sewage,
was another notorious region, a mixture of small factories,
timber-yards, rooming houses, brothels, and tenements,
between the Old Quay in the south and elegant Green Park
and St James Street on the west and east. It too had once
been elegant, or at any rate parts had been, and health
inspectors reported that in some towns the streets would be
considered quite good, but by the end of the eighteenth
century it had suffered a decline and the early Georgian
houses were now occupied by innumerable families, often
four to a house, vagrants, and frequently by pigs as well.
Pig-keeping, already banned in Bristol, might be appropriate to Bladud's city, but it was hardly conducive to good
health, and appears to have been widespread in the poorer
quarters until the latter part of the century. Rehousing in
this area (for people, not pigs) had to wait until 1932 when
the Corporation built the rather graceless Kingsmead Flats,
and major clearance did not come until the bombs dropped
in 1942 and opened the region for post-war building of
flats, offices, and the Technical College in the current
rectilinear style which has provoked as much antagonistic
passion as Smollett's Mathew Bramble felt for Georgian
crescents. But this must be left to the next chapter.

The other patch – and none of these patches was very
large – lay in close proximity to the favoured areas about the
Circus. This was the hillside block which included Morford
Street, Ballance Street and Lampard's Buildings, and it was
noted that when 'scarlatina' struck in 1863 this and the
Avon Street area were the focuses of infection, with the
highest death rates. Hard on the heels of the Dolemeads
Improvement Scheme came one for the Lampard's Buildings
in 1902, but here they faced the brick with stone – and only
did one side of the street. The whole area is now in the

process of demolition and a gleaming cliff of flats in recon-
stituted stone, all sitting under a black hat, has taken the
place of Ballance Street.

If it seems that it is only now that the working class have
entered into the picture it is because history is based on
evidence – and this has been lacking in the previous ages.
But now we have to reckon with the nineteenth century
conscience, and however much post-Freudian generations
may suspect Victorian motives (and there were, in any case,
plenty of Victorians who suspected them), however much
we may detest the unctuous utterings of the age, it is a fact
that there was a greater amount of concern than ever before
about the condition of the poor. This meant the collecting of
statistics, the writing of reports, the calling of meetings and
forming of societies who produced long and solemn reports
of their findings and actions, the writing of letters to the
paper, the publishing of pamphlets, and all the other worthy
activities which Dickens, quite unfairly and quite irresistibly,
pilloried because they seemed to him without passion or
humour or love.

Bath has not been without philanthropy before – there were
the Black Alms and the Blue Alms, Bellot's Hospital, the
Magdalen, the Leper Hospital, the Grammar School and
the Blue Coat School, and there was the Hospital which
became the Royal Mineral Water Hospital, but the three
themes of relief, education, and health were to assume much
greater importance from the end of the eighteenth century.

In 1779, a war-time year of shortages, high prices, and
mob agitation, Bath formed, as did many cities, a Provisions
Committee, which used subscription money to buy coal and
food (much of it rice) for sale at low prices to the needy.
Under various names *ad hoc* committees continued to be
formed in crisis years – as for instance the 'Coal and Potato
Fund' of 1838 and the 'Society for Improving the Conditions of the Working Classes in Bath' which set up soup
kitchens in Chatham Row and Avon Street in the hard
winter of 1858 and served an average of 600 quarts a week

and although the Lock was intended to lead to the Peniten-
tiary they accepted that this would not always be the case.
It has since become a hospital.

Respectable ladies were not forgotten in the nineteenth
century. In 1824 Fletcher Partis left money to establish
homes for 30 'decayed gentlewomen' who were to be aged
over 40, to have a personal income of not less than £25 a
year, to be healthy, bona fide c of E, and daughters or widows
of clergymen, professional men, or 'others of corresponding
rank'. They received a pension of not less than £30 a year
and a home in Partis College, three pleasant Greek-revival
ranges of houses built round a grass court. A non-residential
charity was the Bath District of the National Benevolent
Institute, founded in 1811, which gave pensions to 'dis-
tressed upper and middle class' in three grades according to
previous life-style – £12, £16 and, in exceptional circumstances, a Grade A at £20.

The main relief of the poor was of course by the parish
rate and the parish workhouse. After the Poor Law Reform
Act of 1834 the parishes were grouped into Unions with a
central workhouse which in Bath was erected in 1838 at
Odd Down on the southern hills. Made redundant by the
National Insurance Act of 1948 this large complex of
buildings is now St Martin's Hospital. It had only been
open a year when a Guardian published a vitriolic attack on
the rest of the Board who were, he said, arrogant, full of
self-conceit, and positively encouraging pauperism by the
way they handed out relief. Moreover, the Clerk to the
Union, with the connivance of its Medical Officer, had, he
claimed, absconded with £800 of the parish rates. There
were unmentionables, too. 'Time will not permit me to
describe at any length the unpleasant disclosures made by
the schoolmaster, Mr Harris, respecting the person who
was Matron', he wrote. Unfortunately we have only his side
of the question, and on the whole the workhouse seems to
have been well managed. People did, of course, resent the
rates, and the poor hated the 'Bastilles' which, by the doctrine

of 'less eligibility' were designed to be so spartan as to be a last resort.

You would not die on the diet of two meat-and-potatoes dinners a week, the rest bread and cheese, and breakfasts unvaryingly of bread and gruel, but you would not grow fat – and if you were aged and infirm you just got less of everything except that your old gums were given boiled rice or suet pudding in place of bread at dinner. Great unhappiness was caused by the rigid separation of husbands and wives; 'Christmas Day in the Workhouse', which is now a joke, was originally a moving, if melodramatic, poem about an old woman who died rather than enter the workhouse and face separation. We all know of the plight of children from *Oliver Twist* but Bath was involved in an incident which was sufficiently unusual to receive the attention of *Punch*. In 1857 the manager of the Theatre Royal offered the children a free matinee of *Jack and the Beanstalk*. Gleefully they hurried into their best rags, scrubbed their faces and marched off to the treat. At the door they were turned away – their masters had decided at the eleventh hour that they were to be protected from acquiring 'the habits of early dissipation'.

Wage-earning and self-help were naturally preferred to relief, and the Union set up a pin-factory with pauper labour in Morford Street. It also advertised its labour in the unsuccessful hope of attracting industry. Savings were encouraged by the Servants' Fund (1808), which in 1811 reported that 101 servants, all with good character references, had invested with them, and by the Provident Society (1813), one of the first banks for small savers in the country. The greatest hopes, however, were pinned on education whose influence was then, as now, somewhat over-assessed. Again as today the motives with their consequent aims and objective were mixed and often non-congruent. The 'lower orders' were much feared. Bath was reputed to have one of the worst mobs in England and when a Chartist meeting was held in 1839 six troops of North Somerset Yeomanry were assembled in St James's Square, 130 policemen armed with cutlasses lurked in the Post Office, two troops of Hussars were called in from Frome, 600 special constables were stationed in the Guildhall, and 200 Chelsea Pensioners established in the Market. They were not needed. Indeed, throughout all the political agitations of mid-century the only trouble in Bath was a comparatively mild affair when the Lords rejected the Reform Bill in 1831 and Wilkins, a Twerton mill-owner and Captain of the Bath Troop of Yeomanry, was besieged in the White Hart Hotel on his way to mustering his men against the very serious riots in Bristol. He escaped in civilian clothes and the crowd was dispersed by some two hundred special constables, all being quiet by 2 a.m. Nevertheless, authority remained nervous.

Education, as well as being increasingly required by the economy, was seen as a powerful influence on attitudes and was therefore a prime object of control for any group seeking to secure converts to its own way of belief and behaviour, whether the object was to save souls from damnation or employers from the disobedience of workmen – in some cases it was believed that one led to the other. Whether you believed that a child was fundamentally wicked and could only become good by having the Devil frightened out of him, or fundamentally good and only required to have error pointed out (though possibly forcibly), or that he was fundamentally a thinking machine who only needed to be given facts and logic, you had an idea of what you wanted to turn him into and a belief that this could be done in school. Thus Education was an ideological battlefield with the elementary schools as weapons and since religion by its nature and tradition is deeply concerned with patterns of belief and modes of behaviour it was the Churches which were most prolific in their founding. If the children had been able to understand the flood of phrases which rolled over their heads from distinguished visitors on special occasions, or which appeared in reports and prospectuses, they would doubtless have been astonished at the magnitude of what was supposed to be happening to them. And they, who had not asked to come, were expected to be grateful.

The first new Free School was the Lancasterian (later the Bath and Bathforum) opened in 1810 in Corn Street with 300 children. Joseph Lancaster, a Quaker, in the Borough Road School, London, and Dr Andrew Bell, a Church of England clergyman, in Madras each developed a system of monitorial teaching of a similar type. Lancaster's method was adopted by the British and Foreign School Society (1808) and tended to be associated with Methodist and other Free Churches, while Bell's was used by the National Society for the Education of the Poor on the Principles of the Established Church. Bathforum school was non-sectarian but insisted on religious training and observance (e.g. the C of E had to go to Abbey services) and its secretary chaplain was the Reverend Richard Warner (also an eminent local historian) whose reports were said to be 'able, elegant, and pathetic' (i.e. touching the feelings). Mr Parish was also actively, and financially, interested. The school had a series of disastrous young heads (in 1814 tradesmen in Corn Street complained about the noise the boys made when flogged). In 1821 it had to move to cheaper premises in Walcot Street, and in 1828 a fee of a penny a week was introduced. Fortunes changed with the appointment in 1836 of John Wadsworth at £40 a year 'and the pence', and in 1854 the school moved to new premises in Kingsmead Street, which has now vanished under flats and a car park. Incidentally, a branch school for girls was started in Morford Street in 1813 but it did not last long. In 1885 the Bath-forum school got its first government grant – noting with a touch of bitterness that Church schools had got one in 1833.

Dr Bell's system came to Bath in 1817 with the opening, with a dinner of beef and plum pudding, of the 'New Bath District School' at Weymouth House under the local branch of the National Society. The schoolroom was a remarkable building designed by John Lowder, completely circular, with warm air central heating which was unfortunately not very efficient, particularly in the top storey where the girls were, and was later rebuilt in 1896. It is now demolished. The Branch flourished and rapidly established other schools in the parishes of St James, Lyncombe and Widcombe, Walcot, St Swithin's, Trinity, and St Saviour's. Fees were the usual penny a week, but were doubled in 1861.

The government of the Branch was partly by laymen, partly by ministers of the Church of England, and in 1838–40 the two groups came into head-on collision over policy. The new Rector, the Reverend Law, disapproved of the mode of religious instruction and particularly the books used by the Society and firmly maintained as a principle that Church schools in his parish should be directly and completely under his jurisdiction. The Branch appealed to Headquarters in London. The latter were embarrassed but gave support to their Branch. Many letters passed – long ones from the Society, short ones from the Rector. The lay members, who considered themselves devout Churchmen, were upset by the clash with the clergy, and even more disturbed by Law's proposal to set up his own schools and his refusal to continue 'sermons and collections' for the National schools. Matters were no better when Law was succeeded in the next year by the Reverend W. J. Brodrick (later Viscount Middleton and Dean of Exeter), and in desperation the Branch appealed to the Bishop. The result was the 'Fundamental Laws' of 29 April 1841 in which the Rector and his curates were *ex officio* Vice-Presidents, the Branch remained part of the National Society, religious books in the schools were to be confined to those on the Catalogue of the SPCK, and in any future disputes between Parochial clergy and the other Managers over religious instruction the Bishop was to settle the matter, his judgement being accepted as final. By and large it was a victory for Brodrick but after the heat of battle had died down laity and clergy seem to have worked together amicably and after the 1870 Education Act they made a common front against the competition from the Board schools which were not only financially stronger but tended to drain money from the Church schools, some of whose previous supporters were not prepared to pay both a compulsory Education rate *and* a voluntary contribution. In 1876 was formed a Church School Managers' Union mainly concerned with exhortation and publicity. They had 18 schools, with 4,687 children on the role (average attendance, however, was 3,430), and even with the Government grant, based on good reports from Her Majesty's Inspectors, of nearly £2,500 they were running an annual deficit of some £700 although in spite of this they managed in 1899 to build a large new school for Walcot in Guinea Lane just off the London Road.

For higher education there was still King Edward's which staggered through difficult times to emerge greatly strengthened at the end of the century, and other establishments began to appear. In 1852 the Wesleyan Kingswood school moved from Bristol to large new Gothic revival buildings on the slope to Lansdown and in 1856 another group with a landmark tower appeared nearby. This was the Lansdown Proprietary School, founded by a company, and was for boys. In 1865 it went bankrupt and was taken over as the Royal School for Daughters of Officers of the Army. The architect for both was James Wilson, a local man, who had already designed Cheltenham College. Towards the end of the century two other companies founded a Girls' High School (1876) in Portland Place (it later moved to Lansdown Crescent) and Bath College for boys in the old Sydney Hotel, moving later to above Sydney Gardens. This College was a direct result of the success of the newer Public Schools, notably Clifton, Marlborough and Cheltenham, and the head had been second master at Clifton. It was very successful for a time but financial circumstances forced its closure and the buildings became for a time the Spa Hotel. One company never got its school built and judging from the hysterical tones of the prospectus this was probably a good thing. Queen's College, to be sited near Sham Castle, was intended as a bastion against Roman Catholicism whose activities were giving 'awful warnings of impending evil'. It was perhaps the awful warnings, with their echoes of the 1780 Gordon riots in which the little Catholic church in St James's Place was wrecked, which frightened off subscribers, for in many ways the proposals and the links with Oxford and Cambridge were sound. Whatever the reason, the magnificent 'Saxon' (i.e. Norman) towered and embattled building, whose design by the ubiquitous Wilson had been 'graciously approved and condescendingly accepted' by the Queen, never materialised. Meanwhile the Roman Catholics, who already had their own college for the training of priests at Prior Park (later a boys' school), had been quietly founding their own elementary schools – for girls in 1812, boys in 1815, and infants in 1882 when the schools were transferred to new buildings in Old Orchard Street (now Manvers Hall) and then again in 1882 to new schools by their new Priory and fine and steepled church of St John the Evangelist by South Parade. In 1932 the Priory was handed over to the secular clergy. In 1858 a preparatory school for boys and girls (later a girls' grammar school) started with the establishment of the convent of La Sainte in Pulteney Road.

The State entered the secondary education field with the Act of 1889, and the Corporation erected just north of the Guildhall and encroaching on the market the Bath City Secondary Day School for Boys and Girls, which incorporated a Domestic Science College ('recognised' in 1895). In 1913 the inspectors reported: 'The tone of the school is excellent, and the work has been carried out with efficiency' – although they would have liked more teaching practice.

Education for adults was one of the aims of an important agent of self-help which came from the workers themselves. This was the Co-operative movement which became practicable when the Rochdale pioneers discovered the 'divi'. In the 1860s there were several abortive attempts to begin societies in Bath but the real start was at the then separate industrial village of Twerton where in 1888, inspired by

Benjamin Colbourne, a goods guard on the Midland railway and encouraged by Jonathan Carr the owner of the woollen mills, there was founded the 'Twerton Co-operative Society' which in the following February opened the little one-storey shop they had built on the front garden of 20 Victoria Buildings. By 1914 they had three branches, a coal depot, a choral society, an education committee, and had in 1894 organised a co-operative cabinet-makers business which lasted for several years. Meanwhile Bath had formed its own, smaller society, and in 1922 the two were amalgamated.

To many people today the Co-op is just another shop but to some, and certainly to the founders, it is much more – it is an ideal, nothing less than the realisation in an industrial economy of the brotherhood of man expressed through mutual service and regard for the dignity of all people. In an age whose economy was dominated by the profit motive, where not only the worker but the consumer was exploited, it offered an alternative society, democratically governed and devoted to service rather than profit; as late as 1937 the Bath president, E. G. Haskins, could say that given the will, co-operators could be 'the builders of a new Social Order', an Order based, said Vansittart Neale, one of the Twerton founders and himself the secretary of the Co-operative Union, on 'the conception of workers as brethren – of work as coming from a brotherhood of men associating for their common benefit – who therefore rejected any notion of competition with each other as inconsistent with the true form of society'.

But there were more potent forces at work for democracy. In 1832 a great crowd filled the streets from Sydney Place to the High Common, celebrating the Reform Act which was to remove the election of MPs from the Corporation and give it to nearly 3,000 citizens, 35 per cent of the total adult male population. In November the new electorate sent to Parliament the moderate Palmer and the radical Roebuck, a handsome and fiery man with a programme frightening to the Establishment – the ballot, suffrage to all taxpayers, destruction of monopolies, breaking of closed corporations, removal of monopoly of the Bank of England and of the China trade, abolition of the Corn Laws, of the Assessed Taxes, and of slavery, less money for the armed forces, repeal of the Six Acts, cheap justice, national education, and extension of civil and religious liberty. His attitude to organised religion brought him under suspicion not only from the Established church but also from other sects and he got strong opposition from Dr Jay the famous preacher of the Argyle Chapel. When in 1837 Palmer and Roebuck were defeated by the Tory candidates the *Bath Chronicle* was delighted: 'Never was there a more signal triumph of Conservatism – never has there been a more striking proof of re-action. . . . Bath as been one of the most radical ridden places in the country . . . it has been a battle between Conservatism and unmitigated Democracy.' In 1841 Roebuck was back, but in '47 the Tories put up Lord Ashley, the future Earl of Shaftesbury, who combined a reforming passion with Evangelical fervour and proved more to the taste of the Bath electorate.

Democracy came to the Council after the Municipal Corporations Reform Act of 1835 which not only for the first time made the corporation an elected body (although with aldermen) but extended its jurisdiction to the parishes of Lyncombe and Widcombe, and Bathwick. The Radicals gained a majority but in fact the work went on much as before, the two parties tended to compromise and when in 1848 the Tories were returned there was no noticeable change of policy. Their major concern was in providing services for the expanding town and trying to get some cohesion into a system which had grown up piecemeal during the centuries. For example, the water supply, which was inadequate, was divided between the Corporation and some 20 private companies or individuals, including the Circus company, the Charlcombe Company, the Freemen, Lord Darlington's springs for Bathwick, and Earl Manvers's supply for the Abbey area. In 1851 the Corporation got an

Act to build a reservoir at Batheaston but they were still finding it difficult and in some cases impossible to supply the higher areas – and street watering, very necessary in the days before tarmac, was done with river water, which was far from healthy. In 1870 a new Act enabled them to make considerable extensions. They put in new reservoirs to the north with an 18-in main in the town, and spent nearly £10,000 on buying or renting the various private works. By the '80s they had extended the mains to the suburbs, including the southern hills where the Somerset and Dorset tunnelling activities had diminished the local supply, laid fire mains, and provided adequate supplies for the rapidly increasing number of water closets.

Another problem was the removal of the products of these closets, of the older privies and slop-pails, of the ubiquitous horse, of the 53 slaughter houses, 31 of them in the heart of the city, and of the offal from the butchers' shops which as early as 1778 Thicknesse had complained was polluting the river. With each building development sewers, usually rectangular, of stone or wood, cleaned by opening from the top, had been put in, usually under the cellars, but the Health of Towns Commission noted in 1845 that there were no *public* sewers in the town, and the Bath Health of Towns Association set up in 1847 to publicise the Physical *and Moral* Evils of bad sanitation and 'mal-construction of Dwelling Houses' was urging action. So was Mr Sneade Brown who set himself up as the sanitary conscience of the Corporation and belaboured them with lengthy letters to the newspaper. However, in 1864 the City Engineer, Alfred Mitchell, put forward a plan for an extensive modernisation, including the banishment of pigs, the setting up of public abbatoirs, restrictions on the accumulation of bones and other refuse, streets to be pitched with non-absorbent material, sash windows not to be nailed up, new sewers to be laid, and a 'deoderising plant' to be built. This was approved by the government inspector, loan permission given, and work started. Once again, Bath was entering the modern age, but the system was not adequate and in 1905 the Somerset County Council asked the City to take steps to prevent untreated sewage entering the river. In 1907 the Corporation made a scheme which involved a pumping station at Twerton, a sewage farm at Saltford, the replacement of many old sewers, a main intercepting sewer along the river, and an extension of the Borough to include Twerton, Charlcombe, and part of Weston. They got their extension and in 1914 the new works were declared open.

Following the Health Act of 1875 the 'mal-construction' of houses was combated by by-laws which laid down standards in detail for such matters as width of roads, access to backs, provision of open space and of adequate sanitation, thickness of walls, and fire-risk precautions. This led to large areas, as in Lower Oldfield Park and Bear Flat, being laid out in respectable, if monotonous, terraces.

Two completely new services were gas and electricity and in both of these Bath made an early start – indeed it was the first town outside London to have an electricity company. The large and gauntly impressive gasworks on the Upper Bristol Road, contributing a distinctive flavour to the air, are shortly to be dismantled. Embedded in them is a plain stone building engraved in forthright lettering with the inscription BATH GAS LIGHT AND COKE COMPANY. These offices were erected in 1858–9 and were designed by Manners, but the company had been formed in 1818, in spite of local and Corporation opposition – 'offensive odour, offensive effluvia, foetid fluids, gasometers would blow up, gas lights subject to immediate and simultaneous extinction'. In 1818 they started the gasworks, by the river for coal and coke transport and at that time well outside the built-up area. A contemporary said it looked like a chapel on fire. In 1819 the streets were lit, and they had made a beginning on interiors with demonstrations at the Kingston Rooms and the Guildhall. An Act of 1851 made lighting a Corporation responsibility with the Company as suppliers and when

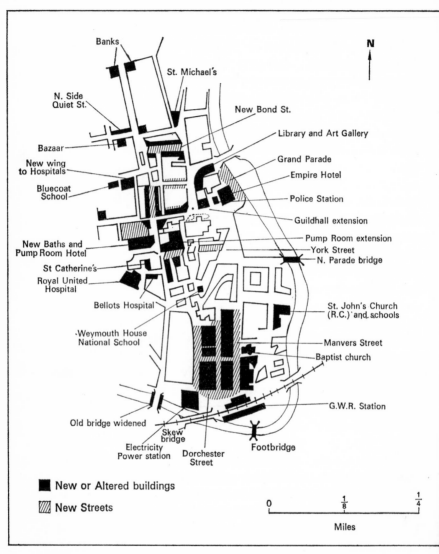

Banks

St. Michael's

N. Side
Quiet St.

New Bond St.

Bazaar

Library and Art Gallery

New wing
to Hospitals

Grand Parade

Empire Hotel

Bluecoat
School

Police Station

Guildhall extension

Pump Room extension

New Baths and
Pump Room Hotel

York Street

N. Parade bridge

St Catherine's

Royal United
Hospital

St. John's Church
(R.C.) and schools

Bellots Hospital

Manvers Street

Weymouth House
National School

Baptist church

G.W.R. Station

Old bridge widened

Skew
bridge

Electricity
Power station

Dorchester
Street

Footbridge

N

■ New or Altered buildings

▨ New Streets

0   ⅛   ¼

Miles

MAJOR NINETEENTH–CENTURY CHANGES TO CENTRAL BATH

the Company sought an Act in 1865 to extend their mains, build additional works, and meter public lamps, they were opposed (unsuccessfully) by the Corporation who objected to certain clauses relating to the price of gas for public lighting. By 1865 the mains had extended to Batheaston and Combe Down, and in 1909 to Newton St Loe, Corston, and Saltford; in the other direction they had reached Box, six miles away.

In 1890 came a rival when Henry George Massingham started an electric power station in Dorchester Street, in addition to his activities in Taunton and Exeter. The next year he was bought out and given a seat on the board of the Bath Electric Light and Engineering Company Ltd. whose directors included Alfred Pitman and Henry Newson Garrett, the proprietor of the Midford Fullers Earth Works, and which was to supply 'electric force' and to fix and maintain 'appliances now known or to be invented'. They rapidly extended the service until most of central Bath was lit with arc lamps and 'incandescent lines' were laid to many houses and public buildings (Hospital, Pump Room, Guildhall, York House, etc.) each of which had its own small transformer to lower the voltage for domestic use. In 1895 the Corporation was considering taking over the supply under the powers of a Board of Trade regulation, and in 1877 a loan for the purchase was sanctioned.

We have seen that the city spread outwards in both terraces and villas and that in the interests of developing a physically healthy society there was legislation to control the form of building. But there were also considerable changes in the core area and over this the Corporation, who owned the land involved, was able to act as a planning authority in fact although not yet in name. Thus we find them laying down details of size and style, which sometimes brought them into dispute with the lessees, sitting in judgement on proposed schemes, putting projects up for public competition, and consulting with architects – particularly at the end of the century with Brydon and with Davis. In all this, then as now, there was no want of interested advice from the citizens.

In 1805 plans were adopted for refacing the varied east side of Stall Street in a uniform and bare simplicity relieved only by shallow Doric pilasters. Rebuilding in this century has left this only on the junction with York Street and in one other shop. The next year they widened the north end of Walcot Street and later, in 1829, did the same for Ladymead where the sudden spread still surprises. This was followed (1806–10) with converting Frog Lane into New Bond Street with Palmer's design of a very plain face to which interest is given by a curved corner and a double line of cornices sweeping upwards at intervals to link the ascending levels. The result is very satisfying, as witness the protests at the recent decision to rebuild. The buildings are not, however, suitable for modern use; ceilings are too high, windows are unsuitably placed, the interiors too labyrinthine, the structure not strong enough. Nos 1–4 were empty from 1936–40 when they were taken over by Plummer Roddis as a store which became increasingly hampered by the layout. Other interesting arrivals were Alfred Taylor (1891), bakers who later established their Red House restaurant there (motto: 'I thank God for Everything'), and a branch in 1901 of Dr Jaeger's Sanitary Woollen System Company.

Other early developments were the removal around 1823–33 of the houses which masked the north side of the Abbey, the making of a carriage-way through York Street (*c.* 1806) south of the Abbey, the construction of the Corridor (Goodridge, 1825), a pleasant, civilised, covered street of shops with gold lion-heads, wreaths, and a music gallery, and the making of Charlotte Street named after Lady Rivers (1839). Charlotte Street was soon crowned with an interesting trio – a Savings Bank (Alexander, 1841), a 'bracket and mantleshelf' Italian Renaissance *palazzio*, rich but not gaudy, and beautifully proportioned; a Moravian (now Christian Science) church in Greek Revival style, very simple and pleasant if not entirely correct (Wilson again,

1824); and a spreading, arcaded, octagonally lanterned chapel, striking in its awfulness (Goodridge, who knew better, 1854).

In the first half of the century over a dozen new churches and chapels were built, nearly all Gothic of one sort or another and few as satisfying as the rarer Grecian examples, the best of which, the Friends' Meeting House in York Street, was actually built as a Freemasons' Hall in 1819. It is by William Wilkins, responsible, amongst other things, for the uncompleted Downing College, Cambridge, University College, London, the National Gallery, and the Gothic screen to King's College, Cambridge. He had studied Greek buildings in Italy, Greece, and Asia Minor and published an influential book, *Antiquities of Magna Graecia* (i.e. Southern Italy) in 1807. The best of the Gothic is St Mary's, Bathwick, although some people have a fancy for the bespired St Michael's (Manners, 1835–7) or light-pierced St Stephen's (Wilson, 1840–5) perched on the Lansdown slopes. St Mary's is by John Pinch the elder, who did good Adamesque work in Sydney Place (1807) and Sion Hill Place (1818–20). In 1815 Bathwick got an Act for the building rate to replace its church which was 'ruinous and decayed' and its workhouse which was not 'proper and commodious'. For Quakers the rate was to be stated in two parts and they could appeal against the church allocation if they wished. Lord Darlington (later Duke of Cleveland) gave the land but money was short and the workhouse was never started – which was fortunate as the new Poor Law made it unnecessary. The church was consecrated in 1820.

The early days also involved the Abbey in the 1833 restoration we have already noted but a much more thorough and correct one followed the inspection and report by Sir G. G. Scott in 1860. It was expensive, particularly in fan-vaulting the nave and like most church building in Bath, was financed entirely by voluntary contributions. Each year the committee set up in 1865 was calling for more money and always their appeals were answered. The Freemasons

paid for the west front, Gore-Langton of Newton Park gave
£100, so did the Duke of Cleveland, Stuckey's Bank gave
£100, so did the Bishop. They and a host of others gave and
gave again – but hundreds of pounds more were given by
the Rector, the Reverend Charles Kemble, who was the
driving force behind the whole operation. The restoration
took ten years and produced a church which could once more
rightly bear the title of 'The Lantern of the West'. In 1895–
1901 the west front was again restored under the direction
of Sir T. G. Jackson who in 1923–6 added a cloister along the
south side. Further renovations were done in 1948–60.

The concern for health which we have already noted also
produced new buildings – an Eye Hospital (1811) in
Lansdown Road, and Ear, Nose and Throat Hospital (1837),
the large new United Hospital (1826, Pinch; Albert wing
added in 1864, Gill), and three dispensaries. In 1830 an
Act was obtained to provide the old General Hospital with
its own baths, filled from the hot springs by a steam pump
whose engine had to 'consume its own smoke'; no longer
were patients to be seen carried in chairs to and from the
Baths. About 30 years later the hospital was doubled in size
by the addition of a second block. Designed by Manners
and Gill, it makes a good neighbour to Wood's original.
Swimming baths for the general public also appeared and
with some modification are used today. In 1815 the Duke of
Cleveland provided an open air bath by the river; the
Corporation bought this in 1860, having already built an
indoor one in 1830 next to the Hot Bath (Decimus Burton;
rebuilt 1859).

But what was particularly noted as 'affording health and
recreation to all classes' was the Royal Victoria Park. In
1839 the Freemen were persuaded to let the 'Common
Fields' to the City at £6 a year; later, by a long and detailed
Act of 1879 the Corporation bought the land in return for
annuities which were paid until 1938 when the last Freeman
died. Lady Rivers, owner of the property around the
Crescent, granted land for an approach road and this, too,

was bought in 1886. About £7,000–8,000 was raised by subscription for laying out the ten-acre site under the direction of the City architect, E. Davis, a pupil of Soane, and father to Major Charles Edward Davis FSA, a later City architect. Urban parks, so much a feature of the nineteenth century were very different from the eighteenth-century Vauxhalls. For one thing they were free and for another they were essentially family places, middle class places, tamed, instructive with their labelled plants, and moral. As towns grew and access to the countryside from the centre became more difficult the presence of these urban lungs became increasingly important and Bath has five, including Hedgemead by the London Road which fills a space created when the buildings skidded on the unstable clays.

In 1830 the Duchess of Kent visited Bath with her 11-year-old 'illustrious and interesting daughter', who on visiting the site 'signified her desire' that it should be named the Royal Victoria Park. Seven years later, when she became Queen, the Park was given gate-piers surmounted by open-mouthed lions from the Masonic Hall presented by Mr Geary. Even more distant from their original destination are a pair of marble vases which were originally designed for Napoleon to give to Josephine.

The nineteenth was a century of Societies where earnest amateurs gathered together to show each other their fossils or read each other papers about their findings and opinions in history, literature, science, theology, or whatever. Bath's quota included a Microscopical Society (which was quite large), a Field Club which regularly published its findings in local history, a Literary and Philosophical Society (1825) and a Literary and Scientific Society (1822). In 1825 also the Mechanics Institute was started in 20 Westgate Street. In 1841 it moved to a site near the Orange Grove and assumed the prestigious name of Athenaeum. It is tempting to think that this represents a triumph for the bourgeoisie, but the matter needs further investigation. In any case it amalgamated with the Institution in 1899.

The Institution was the Literary and Science building in which was established a considerable library and museum with the splendid Moore collection of fossils and rocks which, it is said, all started when the young Charles Moore as a schoolboy at Ilminster rolled a rock down a hill and found a fish inside. The first site for the Institution became available when the Lower Assembly Rooms burnt down in 1821, helped by a lot of paint in store, leaving only the heavy Grecian portico Wilkins had added in 1806. Behind this portico they built in 1825 their home.

The late Victorian and Edwardian period saw something of an economic revival in Bath. This was partly due to increased industrial activity, assisted by increasing national prosperity. In 1870 Bayer's large corset factory in brick was set up next to the flour mills on the Lower Bristol Road, and about the same time Stothert's moved to large new iron-foundry works in the same area, called the Newark Works after their previous place in Newark Street started about 1834, which itself had replaced their 1815 foundry in Southgate Street. Printing (e.g. Pitman's) and bookbinding increased and established a reputation, while light engin-eering came with the establishment of the Horstmann Gear Company in 1902 in James Street West. Just before the First World War and for a short time after they were pro-ducing their own motor cars. In view of the subsequent development of the firms it is interesting to note that in 1802 George Stothert was running an ironmongery business in Horse (Southgate) Street and that in 1879 Gustav Horstmann was making clocks in Bladud Buildings and had patented a perpetual, self-winding clock, while in 1900 Otto Horstmann sold bicycles and optical goods in Rivers Street, and Horstmann and Sons were opticians in Union Street.* Other firms which had arrived by 1900 were Spears, whose pie factory in Philip Street has just been knocked down, a

---

* The actual founder of the new works was S. A. Horstmann, himself an inventor of distinction.

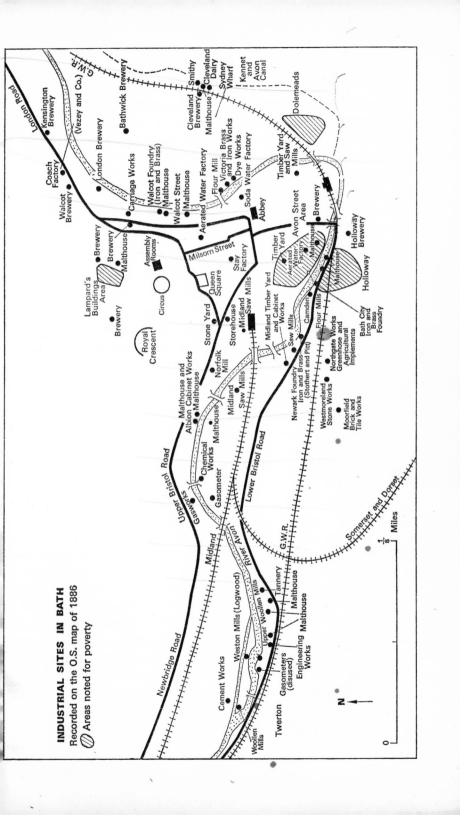

INDUSTRIAL SITES IN BATH

Recorded on the O.S. map of 1886

⬗ Areas noted for poverty

London Road

Kensington Brewery

G.W.R. (Vezey and Co.)

Coach Factory

Walcot Brewery

London Brewery

Bathwick Brewery

Smithy

Cleveland Brewery

Cleveland Dairy

Sydney Wharf

Kennet and Avon Canal

Dolemeads

Carriage Works

Walcot Foundry (Iron and Brass)

Walcot Street Malthouse

Walcot Street Malthouse

Aerated Water Factory

Flour Mill

Victoria Brass and Iron Works

Dye Works

Soda Water Factory

Timber Yard and Saw Mills

Brewery

Holloway Brewery

Brewery

Brewery

Malthouse

Assembly Rooms

Milsom Street

Stay Factory

Timber Yard

Aerated Water Factory

Avon Street Area

Malthouse

Malthouse

Holloway

Holloway

Lampard's Buildings Area

Queen Square

Midland Saw Mills

Midland Timber Yard and Cabinet Works

Camden

Flour Mills

Bath City Iron and Brass Foundry

Brewery

Royal Crescent

Circus

Stone Yard

Storehouse

Midland Mill

Norfolk Mill

Saw Mills

Saw Mills

Newark Foundry Iron and Brass (Stothert and Pitt)

Northgate Works Greenhouse and Agricultural Implements

Malthouse and Albion Cabinet Works

Malthouse

Malthouse

Midland

Saw Mills

Westmoreland Stone Works

Moorfield Brick and Tile Works

Chemical Works

Gasometer

Upper Bristol Road

Gasworks

Midland

River Avon

Lower Bristol Road

G.W.R.

Somerset and Dorset

Newbridge Road

Cement Works

Weston Mills (Logwood)

Upper Woollen Mills

Tannery

Malthouse

Malthouse

Gasometers (disused)

Engineering Works

Twerton

Woollen Mills

N

0   ⅛   Miles

gasfitting works in Monmouth Place, the Railway Ironworks in Railway Place, Midland Engineering (electrical)
in Milk Street, Griffin Engineering at Kingston Ironworks
in Oldfield Road, and the Philosophical Instrument Makers
of Broad Street who turned into opticians.

A more important change, however, was the temporary
revival of spas, following continental initiative. This revival
of 'Balneology' was based mainly on a contemporary fascina-
tion of science and the over-fed, under-exercised condition
of the well-to-do urbanite. The old business of wallowing
about in the water and drinking it in quarts was no longer
good enough. Now you had to have it 'atomised' or 'vapour-
ised' or injected into one of your orifices, or sprayed on you,
or jetted on you, or given to along with electric shocks, and
the Continent must be brought to you in case you were
tempted to go to it. So Bath had to provide the Aix-les-Bains
douche, the Turkish system, the Russian, the Marienbad,
the Vichy, the Mont Doré, and the Auvergne systems, and
even the waters were imported (to Bath of all places!) in case
you wanted them. There had to be an Inhalation Room, a
Humage room (for douching eyes, ears, and throat 'with or
without steam'), and a Spray room; and there had to be Sitz
baths and Needle baths and Atomised Spray rooms. All of
which would have greatly surprised eighteenth-century
bathers and for which the old baths were totally unsuited,
as well as being in 'a state of decay' and 'verging on utter
neglect', as Dr Augustus Bozzi Granville reported on his
tour of British spas in 1841.

The result was that the Corporation bestirred itself and
in 1889 presented visitors with the re-designed King's and
Queen's Baths and a new suite in Bath Street with a Tepid
Swimming Pool and a smoking room. The designs were by
Davis who claimed that they were 'appointed in the best
manner' with appliances providing everything 'from the
simple bath to the most delicate administration of the
Mineral Waters'. The Bath Committee thought he had
spent too much money. The new Queen's Bath was opened

in June 1889 with much celebration including a High Tea in the Drill Hall for 1,500 aged poor. In connection with the new (Royal) Baths the Pump Room Company was started in 1870 and replaced the White Hart with a large hotel redolent of the French Second Empire.

For much of the nineteenth century, as previously, travellers who only stayed for a short time put up at an inn, while people coming for a season would hire a house or apartment. At that time a hotel was a large town house, used by a family for perhaps a season each year. The concept of the purpose-built hotel catering for both long- and short-term visitors was a later development largely connected with the railways, and many hotels are really converted villas. With the revival of the spa there seemed to be good prospects for a new, large hotel, and in 1898 Mr Alfred Holland approached the Corporation with a proposal for what was to be the Empire Hotel in Orange Grove. This fitted well, as he knew, with a scheme the Corporation had been considering for many years of cutting a new carriage-way from Pierrepont Street to Bridge Street via the Orange Grove and the then New Market Place, and he was happy to fit in with this, using a 'Jacobean' design by Davis, and adding that he was 'taking it for granted there are no restrictions as to height'. Agreement reached, the Corporation was going ahead when it hit two snags. The first, fairly easily dealt with, was the objection by John Wood, a descendant of his architect namesake, that the Corporation were proposing, without prior consultation, to use a piece of his land. The other, which made them shift the line of the road, was a clause they had overlooked in Earl Manvers's conveyance of the land which is now the Parade Gardens. The result was a complete re-modelling of the area into what we see today, with the balustraded Grand Parade standing on a colonnade where once was a clutter of markets, and the overpowering bulk of the Empire Hotel with its curious skyline of assorted gables and castellations.

This was in fact all part of a great change which the

Corporation was making to the structure and appearance of central Bath. The Roman Baths were now revealed, a source of civic pride and a potential money-spinner, requiring some sort of setting. Moreover the new style of spa needed an entertainment centre or, as the newspapers called it, a Kursaal. Also the increasing complexity and responsibility of local government required much more accommodation than the Guildhall could provide. In 1891 the Corporation therefore established a committee which set a competition for plans for an extension to the Guildhall and an addition to the Pump Room which would include a concert hall, a suitable setting for the Roman remains, and a Museum. The architect appointed in 1892 was J. McKean Brydon (a Scotsman who was working for the Local Government Board in Whitehall) and it is interesting to see that the Corporation specified that the new work should harmonise with the old and that they chose designs which were neither Grecian nor Gothic but which harked back to the days of Palladian Bath, albeit with touches of the Baroque. Brydon's work is heavier than Baldwin's but it conforms without imitating and the result is that both the old Guildhall and Pump Room sit very easily with the additions of nearly a century later. His first design for the Kursaal would not have been so satisfactory for it continued the Pump Room along in one monumental block which would have swamped the old and created scale problems. The Roman baths were in this design to have been roofed with 'iron principles covered with red Italian tile', but in the second version were left open and surrounded by a colonnade topped with statues by Lawson, who also did the sculptures on the Guildhall.

Bath still lacked what every city of Victorian pride was acquiring, a library and art gallery, and this was the more surprising as the city counted itself a cultural centre and looked with some satisfaction on the long list of literary and artistic people who had been connected with the place. Various schemes were proposed and came to nothing and

33 The New Bath, 1889 (now replaced by a neo-Georgian block)

34 'Isaac Pitman, his mark'

KINSTON BILDINZ

35 Brydon's first design for the Pump Room extension and Roman Baths

36 Brydon's Guildhall extension

then, as the prospect of celebrating the Diamond Jubilee
was creating excitement, Mrs Arabella Roxburgh left a
large bequest for schools and for the founding of an Art
Gallery; moreover the money had to be used in five years.
Given this spur at such an opportune moment, and heartened
by a further donation of £1,000 from H. O. Wills, the
Corporation decided that there should be a gallery and a
library, and that a competition should be held amongst Bath
architects only. On second thoughts and under the pressure
of some local opinion they decided to hand the job over to
Brydon. He gave them a rather splendid building with a
dome at one end, a marble foyer, large windows, and a series
of blank niches for statues of notabilities connected with
Bath and an ornate one in the middle for the Queen. The
niches remain empty, except for a regal statue of Victoria
presented by the Bath ladies. Unfortunately it took a long
time to realise the project and it had to be put in as a
memorial. The library was for reference only and it was not
until 1924 that a lending department was incorporated. The
building may not be adequate by modern standards for
showing art, and the reference library had to be moved out
to Queen Square in 1959, but the building was a satisfying
addition to the townscape. The foundation stone was laid
and the Pump Room extensions opened in blazing sunshine
in Jubilee Year, 1898, by His Royal Highness the Duke of
Cambridge. He did not have much to do with politics, he
said (laughter), but he believed in the Empire (applause),
his theme being that it was all very well to get an Empire
or a Kursaal, the real job was keeping it a going concern.
The Art Gallery was opened in 1900. The weather was fine
and the Lady Mayoress looked splendid in a heliotrope dress
and a black hat with ostrich feathers, but the bunting (not
on the Lady Mayoress) could have been more lavish.

Building the Guildhall extension had deprived William
Henry Smith of his leather shop so when it was proposed to
rebuild the corners of Cheap Street he had priority for the
High Street end, which is why 'WHS 1895' is to be seen on

the corner; by a stroke of irony the shop is now occupied by Curry's who were displaced by the demolition of Southgate Street in 1972 for rebuilding. Before this, in 1885 the Westgate Street/Union Street corner had been rebuilt. In 1870 Colmer's filled most of one side of Union Street with a Baldwinesque design and in 1871 Davis put a new façade on the north side of Quiet Street, opposite Goodridge's Bazaar of 1824. In Milsom Street two ornate banks appeared at the top corners in 1865 and '75, large shop fronts such as Jolly's (1879) were put in, and the back gardens on the west covered by rearward shop extensions. The full story of these street changes has yet to be told, and merits a separate book, but one of the recurrent characteristics is an increase in size and a passion for ornament which may cause some disruption of the scene and yet because Bath stone was used and because the architects had some respect for the eighteenth-century idiom is acceptable and indeed unnoticed by most people.

One building difficult to ignore is Beckford's Tower on Lansdown hill (Goodridge, 1826–7). William Beckford was the son of a Lord Mayor of London who had made a fortune from property in the West Indies. When his father died the ten-year-old William was a millionaire. In 1784 at the age of 24 he became MP for Wells but his mind was fantastical and politics bored him. Gothick and Eastern fancies preoccupied him. He wrote an Eastern novel, *Vathek*, in French, and in 1795 set about building what was virtually a gigantic summer house, Fonthill Abbey, with a tower nearly 300 feet high. If a Bath resident, Mrs Ratcliffe, wrote novels which seem now to inspire Hammer Films, Beckford was a precursor of darkest Disneyland. What he sought, and what he got, was the 'sublime', awesomeness, mysteriousness, light and shadow, and immense size. And then he lost a great deal of money, sold his Abbey, and in 1822 retired to Bath with his devoted servant. Three years later the Abbey tower fell down, certain important matters such as foundations having been inadequately seen to. He bought two houses in Lansdown Crescent, joined them with a bridge, bought the land up to Lansdown top and there had a new tower, a good deal smaller and more substantial, but a notable landmark, designed by Goodridge, from which on a clear day he could see the ruins of Fonthill. He did not go out much, but might sometimes be seen riding very slowly on his horse, followed by a groom with a bag of pennies for distribution. If he happened to dismount the groom would take his place, presumably to keep the saddle warm. In his last few years he became a complete recluse but when he died in 1844 at the age of 85 Bath saw one of its most magnificent funerals. His daughter, the Duchess of Hamilton, gave the tower and cemetery to the Rector of Walcot and the church has only just managed, in 1972, to get rid of it.

Beckford was a national figure, one of the great eccentrics, and books have been written about him. In the late nineteenth century Bath had a man of even wider repute, and for more solid reasons, Sir Isaac Pitman, or as he would have preferred it EIZAK PITMAN. Born at Trowbridge in 1813, he taught at Barton-on-Humber and then Wooton-under-Edge where he became interested in phonetics. In 1844 he wrote his little grey fourpenny book on Stenographic Sound-Hand and printed it in his own house. Next year he gave up teaching to devote his life to the propagation of his ideas on reformed spelling and shorthand, and acquired some premises in Albion Place on the Upper Bristol Road, which became the FONETIC INSTITUWEON and PRINTIŊ OFIS. The project prospered. In 1855 he moved to Parsonage Lane and then in 1874 to KIŊSTON BILDIŊZ where the phonetic name can still be seen. The name Pitman had become synonymous with shorthand and his fame was international. Printing was taking place in London, but Bath remained the headquarters and in 1889 the works and offices moved to buildings designed by J. Willcox on the Lower Bristol Road where, with later modifications, they remain. In 1894 Isaac Pitman was knighted. He was never involved in civic affairs, although often invited to stand for Council, but was active in the cause of temperance, of co-operation, and, early converted to the tenets of Swedenborg, was a faithful attender, organist, and preacher at the New Church off Manvers Street, and possibly another in Twerton popularly known as 'the Pitman chapel'. In 1896 he died at his home, 17 Royal Crescent, which was later marked by a commemorative tablet, although some people argued that it would be more appropriate on Albion Place.

These tablets were the idea of T. Sturge Cotterell and the first one, to Herschel, was put up in 1898: they certainly add interest to a walk round Bath even if we cannot always be certain that they are on the most appropriate building – or even, very occasionally, the right one – the Gainsborough plaque has just been moved.

In spite of strenuous publicity Sir Isaac's new alphabet never caught on; a total reorganisation of spelling would have meant too big a disorganisation of established practice. His great-grandson Sir James Pitman has, however, had considerable success with an alphabet which is not intended for general use but to enable children to get away to a faster start in learning to read. This is i.t.a., the initial teaching alphabet, and although arguments both for and against appear inconclusive, it has, like so many educational experiments, worked well when administered by teachers who are enthusiastic for it.

In conclusion, we shall consider an incident which was entirely, and some might say peculiarly, a Bath matter. Major Charles Edward Davis both as City Architect and in private practice made considerable contributions to Victorian Bath, but many of his actions aroused controversy and perhaps none so much as the question of the City Arms. From the sixteenth century the accepted Arms of Bath have appeared in maps and manuscripts and graven in stone as a shield with wavy lines surmounting a battlemented wall, usually with two loops and a vertical sword, occasionally with a key on it – technically 'per fesse embattled azure and gules, the base masoned sable with crosses boutonnee of the last in chief two bars wavy argent, over all in pale a sword of the last hilt and pommel or'. It is taken to signify a walled city with bathwater. The sword might refer to the Romans, or to St Paul, and the key might be put in to placate St Peter although its insignificant size seems inappropriate.

In 1888 Davis produced a different version and, without seeking authority, took down the arms from the Guildhall pediment and substituted what was virtually the old arms upside-down, and without loopholes. The significance was quite different for by putting the wall at the top the 'battlements' became recesses in the side of a bath. Davis, as an antiquary, maintained that these were the official arms because they were the only ones recorded at the College of Heralds, although there had never been any grant of arms to the city at any time, and the recorded arms were simply part of a report of Visitation in 1623. Davis was made to replace the old arms, but the Corporation and many citizens were now ranged in two camps, one under the Customary Arms and the other under the Visitation Arms.

The Corporation, by a majority, applied to the College of Heralds for confirmation of the Customary Arms, but the opposition sent in a Counter Memorial which created further confusion. What really seems to have restrained the Corporation from pressing the matter to a conclusion was that the College was only prepared to make a grant of the Customary Arms as a new one dating from 1889 and this seemed to many to be unsatisfactory if not positively insulting. The Corporation therefore took the simple line that the City had produced its own arms, had used them for centuries, and that they were going to go on using them. The matter of confirmation was raised again in 1953, when in answer the Corporation issued a booklet giving the history of the affair; and now in 1972 it has been decided to petition the College for confirmation of the Customary Arms. An additional suggestion that it would be more appropriate to have a full coat of arms is interesting as the 1953 booklet suggested that one way out of the difficulty of a *de novo* grant might be met by applying for 'a Grant of Supporters by way of embellishment of the ancient Arms of the City'.

But why in 1623 did the Heralds record something different from the Customary Arms? The most probable explanation is that they were given them by the Chapmans, of whom we have already heard, for they stayed at the White Hart which was then occupied by Walter Chapman and whose family produced a genealogy which included 'the proper insignia for the Seal of the Mayor, Aldermen, the Citizens of Bath' (the Visitation Arms), and Arms used in ignorance (the Accepted Arms). But they had not invented them, the monks had. If we look at the bosses of the Abbey nave we shall see that two are decorated with the Visitation Arms, although the Accepted Arms are blazoned over the crossing. Now the nave bosses date from Scott's restoration but it is highly improbable that he invented them, and the monkish origin is strengthened by the Red Book of Bath, which Davis did not know about, where in a fifteenth-century poem about King Arthur appears a rough sketch of the *Escu du Baa* which seems almost certainly the forerunner of the 1623 Arms. In using *du* instead of *de* the title suggests Arms of the Baths rather than of Bath, and it seems very possible that at one time there were two shields, one for the monastery and one for the City, in which case there may have been monkish chuckles in Heaven, for the Battle of the Arms becomes a descendant of their own Battle of the Bells.

To many the controversy may seem trivial but it is indicative of that fierce pride in the history of their City that gave energy, as it still gives energy, to action. And with it in Victorian times was coupled sheer nerve, for it was nerve which drove through the changes of the age at a time when prudence would have dictated retrenchment. We may not think that what they did was the best, but they did at least act. It was a disgrace to their city to have poverty, beggars, bad drains, poor water supply, ignoble streets, lack of education, inadequate transport, neglected baths, a cluttered and rotting Abbey – and so many things were done, usually in an atmosphere of battle, reported by a lively and interested press which had no hesitation about joining in, for editors, too, loved Bath.

And perhaps one of the most notable examples of nerve was the great Bath Pageant of 1909. There were plenty to forecast that it would be a disaster. It was a waste of the ratepayers' money; people were tired of pageants and would not come; the project would not appeal to the citizens and there would not be enough contributions either in money or effort; and so on! Arguments in favour were that it would be a splendid advertisement, encourage the tourist trade, especially the Americans, and that Cheltenham had made a substantial profit on their Pageant the year before, but these were not the real reasons which drove the matter through and fired the imagination of a city. Of course it could have been a flop – a week of bad weather alone could have ruined it – and so it took nerve to go ahead, as it had taken nerve for the young Wood to press on with the schemes which some thought 'chimerical'. In the event it was all a great success. In the bright summer light of July some 3,000 actors, an orchestra of over 70, a choir of over 300, real pigs for Bladud and real horses for the Cavaliers and Roundheads, everybody in costume, played out on the green grass of Victoria Park before packed houses the story of their city. It was written by local people, produced by local people, played by local people. Only for the last month did they bring in a professional Pageant Master, Frank Lascelles, who brought the whole thing together, using a high tower and field telephones. Civic dignitaries were invited from Canada and America, and came; the London press were invited, and came; the Duke of Connaught was invited to open the Pageant, and he did. And at the end of each night, as the shadows lengthened and the grass dampened, and the thousands gathered to say farewell, a sort of magic must have invested a scene which sounds perhaps naïve, even banal, in the script:

Bells ring, cannons boom, doves fly up, the people cheer, MOTHER BATH is covered with a shower of roses from the thousands of her sons and daughters of all time, and as they bear her away with them the strains float up of 'O God our help in ages past'.

Five years later the country was at war.

9 New Wine in Old Bottles

The Twentieth Century

The First World War was traumatic. It shook the fabric of a society from which a generation fell to death. It shook the structure of the economy so fiercely that no plan to mend, amend, or reform appeared to have the power to set it right. It shook accepted beliefs. And above all, it shook nerve. Everything seemed to have been thrown into the melting pot, and the pot was stirred by fear. Fear and hatred. Fear and hatred of war, fear and hatred of unemployment, fear and hatred of the bosses, of the workers, of the other men going for the one job. Two million unemployed in 1921, nearly three million in 1932 (23 per cent of all insured workers), still over one and three-quarter million in 1938 on the eve of war. The dole, the Means Test, the hunger marches, the Geddes axe on Government expenditure. The General Strike. The Great Depression, when in three years British exports dropped by nearly half. And abroad the rising tide of totalitarianism.

This popularly held view is incomplete and to many of us who grew up in the inter-war years, particularly in the south-west away from the centres of heavy industry, it may seem almost unrecognisable, for in spite of the times there was something sturdy, indestructible, commonsensical in the British people which fortified them in hard times, which kept them from extremes of action, and which gave them the hope that the reward of tenacity would be revival. And revival there was, for in the later thirties the economy was beginning to strengthen and new technologies were extending higher standards of living further and further down the income scale. Nor was it solely a time of retrenchment – there were forward movements in education, in housing, in transport, in rebuilding our towns, in social insurance and in the beginnings of planning. There were still, of course, huge areas of under-privilege, but in general the standard of living was rising and when the country entered once more upon war it was with no sound of trumpets, for this conflict was seen not as a means of glory but as an unpleasant necessity, adding, as it were, the burden of mending our fences and helping our neighbours at a time when we had just begun to see our own house getting into order.

It is the gentler picture that we see when we look at inter-war Bath. The city shared in the national problems but its difficulties, real enough to its citizens, were on a minor scale compared to the catastrophic conditions in South Wales or Tyneside. When Neville Chamberlain visited Bath as Minister of Health in 1932 he told the Mayor that relatively speaking the city had no slums. Tactless as usual, he was however, by national standards, right. This comparative advantage had its drawbacks for it put the city very low on the government's priority list for financial aid, with the result that although Bath planned with vigour only a proportion of the schemes came to fruition.

These included improvements in water, sewerage, fire service (with a new station by Cleveland bridge in 1938), street lighting (with the important decision to adopt sodium lamps whose amber glow adds grace to the city at night), and a considerable expansion in education. Two Grammar Schools were built, one for boys and one for girls, a new Infants School was built in the growing area of Southdown, and when in 1932 the Royal United Hospital moved to the site of the war time hospital at Combe Park its old building was occupied by the Technical College whose Principal was also Director of Education for the City. In 1921 Oldfield Boys' and Girls' Schools became Senior Schools. On the other hand the period saw the end of Bathforum School (1926) and the Bluecoat School.

Although the total population of Bath declined slightly during this period there was a considerable demand for housing and the Corporation was dominant in this field, partly with the powers and financial assistance under the old Working Class Act, but mainly under Addison's Act of 1918, the less generous Chamberlain's Act of 1923 and Greenwood's slum clearance Act of 1923. Between the wars they built some 2,000 houses in estates mainly on the upper slopes and top of the southern plateau but with some on the western terraces above the Avon (see map, p. 192). Thus imbued with the prevalent Garden Suburb *ethos*, they added to urban Bath a suburban boxes-and-gardens fringe indistinguishable from the same thing in hundreds of other places except perhaps for the uniformity of material – Bath stone facings and dark roofs (except for one rash of red). Partly because of topographical restraints, partly because of the *rus in urbe* ideal, there is a tendency for roads to curve, but the curves reveal no surprises. One councillor hoped the Corporation would not continue its previous method of designing one house and then repeating it a hundred times. He was not quite fair – they usually designed two houses, one with a parlour and one without. In any case there was a precedent for using a stereotype: Wood had done it, designing houses of First, Second, or Third Rank, the difference being that he stitched them together with genius. The biggest criticism of council estates, not just in Bath but throughout the country, was that they lacked social facilities. Indeed, without cars many people felt themselves isolated from the life of the city and too far from work.

One answer to isolation was to build tenements on cleared slum land, and in 1932 Kingsmead Flats were opened – all £64,000 worth of them. It had been a struggle to get the scheme through and the speeches showed natural pride in

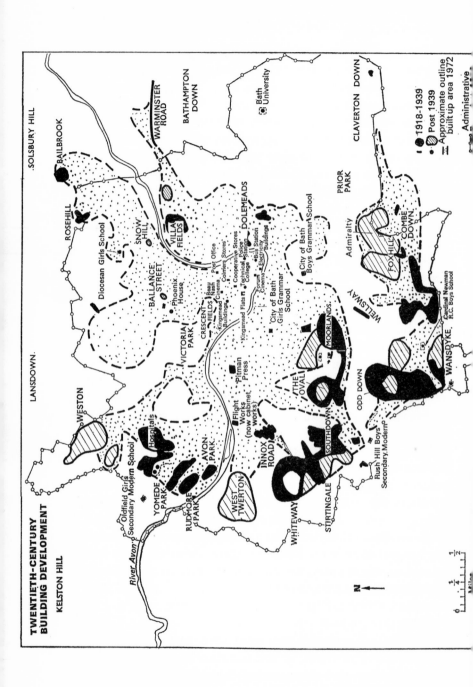

TWENTIETH-CENTURY
BUILDING DEVELOPMENT

KELSTON HILL

LANSDOWN.

SOLSBURY HILL

BAILBROOK

ROSEHILL

WESTON

Diocesan Girls School

SNOW HILL

VILLA FIELDS

WARMINSTER ROAD

BATHAMPTON DOWN

Bath University

Oldfield Girls Secondary Modern School

Hospitals

YOMEDE PARK

RUDMORE PARK

AVON PARK

WEST TWERTON

INNOX ROAD

WHITEWAY

STIRTINGALE

SOUTHDOWN

ODD DOWN

Rush Hill Boys Secondary Modern

VICTORIA PARK

BALLANCE STREET

Phoenix House

CRESCENT FIELDS

Beau Nash

Post Office

Kingsmead Cinema

College
Colonnade Stores

Cooperative Stores

Kingsmead Flats

Technical College

Police Station

Bus Station

Electricity Buildings

Forum Cinema

DOLEMEADS

City of Bath Boys Grammar School

City of Bath Girls Grammar School

Pitman Press

Flight Works (now cabinet works)

THE OVAL

MOORLANDS

WELLSWAY

Admiralty

PRIOR PARK

CLAVERTON DOWN

FOX HILL

COMBE DOWN

WANSDYKE

Cardinal Newman R.C. Boys School

N

0   ¼   ½   1
Miles

River Avon

● 1918-1939
◗ Post 1939
‐‐‐ Approximate outline built up area 1972

Administrative

describing the electric lighting, the choice of heating by gas or coal, the clothes lines (Mondays and Tuesdays), the hygienic rubbish chutes, the boiler in the kitchen from which hot water could be pumped to the bathroom, the separate wcs, the soundproofing, and the verandahs which were 'the tenants' streets'. Meanwhile a private organisation, the Bath Tenements Venture had in 1923 bought the lease of Chandos House, which Wood had built for the Duke, and converted it into little flats. Encouraged by their success they bought houses in Abbeygate Street, turned them into two- or three-room flats and in 1926 let them at 3s 6d a room per week.

The Kingsmead project had been included as part of a major City Improvement scheme for it was felt that by itself it would not attract Government aid. This scheme was put up as a Private Bill in 1924 and became the Bath Act in the following year. It authorised 19 different Works and empowered the Corporation to control hoardings, lay down regulations for one-way traffic, control building styles and materials, and provide what were to be 'hereinafter called parking-places'. It also empowered them to buy the toll bridges and free them in seven years, which they did. Local opposition to the Bill was strong, particularly from the Bath branch of the Citizens' Union who objected that some business men would lose their premises, others would be destroyed, and people from the 'so-called slums' would be left unhoused. One person warned that although Bath 'had benefited from the War as a spa and residential town' there might be difficult times ahead and it was foolhardy to enter on expensive schemes. Petitions against the Bill were sent by two of the bridge companies, the Hospital of St John, the United Hospital, George's Brewery, the Bath Gas Company, three railway companies, and Messrs Bush. So the Corporation held a poll. About 6,000 citizens voted in favour and 4,000 against and although the Citizens' Union claimed only about a third of those eligible had voted, and continued their opposition, the Bill went through, various concessions being made to the counter-petitioners; Mr Bush, for example, who had a well-known shop on the corner of Westgate Buildings, was given temporary accommodation on Kingsmead Square.

Although the economic situation prevented anything like the full implementation of the scheme and lost the city a fine riverside promenade and sweep of buildings in fashionable Municipal Georgian a good deal was done. St James's Parade, for example, was extended to join Southgate Street, with the large Forum Cinema on one side and a range of shops on the other, corners in Kingsmead Square were rebuilt, the old Lit. and Sci. Institute was removed, to the regret of many, the Society transferring to what is now the Reference Library in Queen Square, and the Institute surrounds were refashioned and disembowelled to make public lavatories. In 1932 the Corporation Electricity Company pulled down the Full Moon Hotel and built itself large new offices and showroom (W. A. Williams),* while private enterprise injected more neo-Georgian blocks in the streets: Burton's, for example, remodelled a corner of Stall Street in 1928 (it is now John Collier's), Woolworth's did the same opposite (now electricity showrooms, but the little stone shield on the corner still bears a heraldic W), and in Westgate Street appeared the Beau Nash Cinema which, unlike the Forum, has not yet succumbed to Bingo. The Post Office made its own Classical contribution on the corner of New Bond Street and won national acclaim for it – some may wonder why.

In 1937 the Corporation put up another Bill, met the usual opposition, had another poll, and again got its Act. The biggest opposition had been to the widening of part of Walcot Street but in fact the major scheme was to build a new Royal Mineral Water Hospital. In 1887 Queen

---

* They received a grant from the Unemployment Grants Committee on condition that they employed at least fifteen men from the Employment Exchange and completed the work in a year.

Victoria agreed to change the name of the Hospital to the Royal Mineral Water Hospital, in 1935 George v agreed to the Royal National Hospital for Rheumatic Diseases, down by Avon Street where now the post-war Technical College building stands defying with slit eyes and flat face the wrath of quite a number of Georgian-minded Bathonians. Imminent and actual war called a halt to the development but the Act included a section in which Bath anticipated national legislation by a quarter of a century. This was the listing of buildings, a system which did not become general until the Planning Act of 1962. Under the 1937 Bath Act buildings of architectural importance before 1820 were listed by a panel of two architects, two surveyors, and two JPS and could not be altered without Corporation approval.

The listing of buildings, the perpetuation of a Georgian style, and the restrictions on the use of 'foreign' building materials, were all part of an effort to preserve the special atmosphere of Bath. In the wider environment of the city action was taken under the Town and Country Planning Act of 1932 when on the 23 October 1933 there was a meeting of representatives from the Somerset County Council, the Bath City Council, and the Bathavon Rural District Council. Invitations to Wiltshire and Bradford-on-Avon were declined. A Planning Area consisting of Bath and a large portion of Bathavon was set up, with Bath City Council as the Authority promoting the Scheme. This was approved by the Ministry in March 1934, and in the meantime the authorities concerned gave their Planning Committee executive powers. The major scheme was produced in 1939 and has been superseded by post-war planning, but there was also a good deal of interim development control. Conceived in terms of the relevant Acts and in accordance with planning theory of the time, it was largely a force of negation, but it had one very important outcome: it preserved the green hill setting of the city and ensured an almost complete Outer Green Belt. For example, when a private building scheme was proposed for the Lansdown slopes, it was rejected by the Council. The developers appealed but the decision was upheld.

One of the unfulfilled projects of 1937 was the provision of a large bus station, and this is indicative of an important factor in the economic development of Bath. With the increasing use of buses, cars, delivery vans and ambulances, the city was able to extend its sphere of influence as a service centre, with a consequent increase in importance of shops and stores and of professional services, particularly in the field of medicine, surgery, and psychiatry where consultants now feel the position threatened by proposed changes of local government boundaries. Nor was water treatment neglected: Wood's old Royal Bath building was redesigned inside (in neo-Georgian, of course) by A. J. Taylor, architect to the Baths Committee, and re-opened in 1927 to provide Plombières douches whose enigmatic name cloaked the delicate process of intestinal irrigation.

Meanwhile there was a modest expansion of industry. Stothert's, Hortsmann's, and Pitman's all developed new premises or added to their old ones. The 'Flight Works', an aircraft factory started during the Great War, became Lock's Cabinet Works. Garages were proliferating. Malting and milling, corsetry and clothmaking, books and biscuits, building and baking, all continued to give employment, and there was still a good demand for domestic and hotel service. A notable feature was the increase of female employment in industry.

Unemployment was, of course, a real hardship to many — Bath had 1,407 in 1932, about seven per cent of the local insured workers, and a peak of 2,739 in 1932. This meant work for the Assistance Board and the Mayor's Employment Scheme, by which, it was claimed, a shilling contribution meant an hour's work for an unemployed man, but in general, and in comparison with many other places, the situation was not serious. The city continued steadily as a spa; the visitors' lists show full hotels, there was something of a boom as late as 1937, and even the General Strike of

37 Bath chairs outside the Pump Room, 1912

38 Horse tram in the London Road

39 Tram in Westgate Place, 1925

40 Inter-war Neo-Georgian: the
Forum Cinema

1926 caused only a temporary reduction of ten per cent. The Strike year started with a 'Constant Reader' asking 'When were the majority of the people better clothed or fed; or when was more attention given to the poor and needy?' – a question typical of the attitude to the unemployment situation of many of the securer classes. In February the paper ran a short article on the possible effects of a General Strike, and on 4 May appeared an emergency edition headed GRIP OF THE STRIKE. The transport workers were out, the builders were out, the printers were out, industry by industry, partly or wholly, the men and the women were coming out. Beer was running short. Strike Headquarters had been set up in Green Park station and various Unions were making their own headquarters in buildings about the town. The Mayor addressed a meeting of strikers in the Sawclose, without effect or incident. Bakers sent a car to Harwich to fetch yeast. Volunteers were called for to help run transport and a reporter noted that a lorry driver was seen to be wearing spats. Coal was fixed at 2s 6d a cwt. and people were urged not to stockpile food, in reference to which the paper told a little story. A lady, they said, went into a Bath shop 'in a flurried state' and said that in view of the situation she must do some extra shopping. 'I want', she said, 'six bottles of gin, 12 bottles of port, 12 bottles of whiskey, and enough syphons of soda.' 'Will that be all, madam?', asked the shopman. 'Yes,' said the lady, '– for today.'

The strike ended on the 14th, although on the coalfields the miners hung on for another six months. Traumatic as the experience had been for labour relations as a whole, it left little mark on Bath which rapidly returned to normal, and to its concern with local affairs, one of which was the provision of a swimming pool or Lido, something which has been engaging their attention ever since without anything actually being built. The owner of the Scala cinema in Oldfield Park proposed one next door but it came to nothing. Nor did the scheme to use Twerton gaol. A site on Crescent Fields was proposed but the scheme was defeated by the opposition of the local residents, one of their more imaginative objections being that 'a large sheet of water might provide a splendid guide to aircraft intending to bomb the gas-works'. This was in 1937. In 1939 the Corporation proposed to press on with comprehensive improvement schemes for the City but were warned that Air Raid Precautions would probably involve them in heavy expenditure. In that year came the war, the evacuated children, and the Admiralty. On Saturday, 25 April 1942, came the midnight bombs. Altogether there were three raids, two that night and another, shorter but more intense, the following night. They killed 417 people, injured hundreds more, and destroyed or damaged over 1,900 premises, including the south-east part of Queen Square, the eastern range of Green Park, the Assembly Rooms, St James's church (and others – the bombs were strictly non-denominational), and houses in the Circus and Crescents. The west wing of the Royal Hospital sustained a direct hit. There was heavy damage in the south, in the Kingsmead Street, Avon Street, and Railway Street areas. This 'Baedeker' raid, like the retaliatory bombing of Dresden, was intended to overwhelm with horror. It served to strengthen resolve.

In 1943, when the end of the war was by no means in sight, the Bath and District Joint Planning Committee commissioned Professor Patrick Abercrombie, internationally renowned expert and incredibly prolific producer of imaginative, factually-founded plans and surveys, to advise them on the future development of the City, and in January 1945 appeared A Plan for Bath. Based on an impressive quantity of factual material collected by officers of the Council, the scheme was detailed, imaginative, and expensive. Unlike his London plan, it never got off the drawing board. Amongst other things it would have moved the Council offices to the Royal Crescent, put a Lido in the Recreation Ground, created a shopping precinct along Kingsmead Street, with a new Technical College at the end, made a Health Centre around a new Royal National Hospital

to the east of Green Park, and provided a new hotel and a
large concert hall to the west of Pierrepont Street. Residential areas would have been organised into 14 neighbourhood
areas, each with its own shopping, social, and recreational
centre, all with Junior schools, and eight of them with
secondary schools, single-sex and with not more than four
hundred pupils each. There would have been five new road
bridges over the Avon and a revised road network linked
together with a dozen new roundabouts, a peculiarly British
way of inducing traffic thrombosis.

Abercrombie saw clearly the nature of the traffic problem,
but he did not anticipate its magnitude. In his opinion a
motorway to the north of Bath, proposed in 1938 (and
opened in 1972 as the M4) would not obviate the need for
bigger roads through the City, although he did not think
that Bath itself would need a motorway. What he proposed
were two-lane, 60-foot wide 'arterial roads' – which would
hardly have coped with the present situation. He did not
think a by-pass practicable and proposed that a new road
should enter from the east, south of the London Road and
crossing the river twice, follow Julian Road north of the
Royal Crescent, run along the north side of Victoria Park
and down its west side to cross the river and join the Lower
Bristol Road at a six-road intersection. Another part of the
scheme has actually been carried out, linking the road from
the south into the Lower Bristol Road by a roundabout
which uses arches in the Railway bridge and leads to a
resited Old Bridge (now called Churchill Bridge).

Even if his road plan had been implemented it would have
been no more than a mild palliative, for post-war Britain
was entering upon such an environmentally frightening
increase in road usage that even the Government was
alarmed and in 1960 appointed Colin Buchanan, then
working for the Ministry of Town and Country Planning,
to prepare a Report. This concerned itself not just with
keeping the traffic moving, but also with the effects on the
urban environment. Of historic towns Buchanan wrote:

'There is a great deal at stake: it is not a question of retaining a few old buildings, but of conserving, in the face of the onslaught of motor traffic, a major part of the heritage of the English-speaking world, of which this country is the guardian' – and this was the man Bath Corporation commissioned to 'consider the traffic problems of the city as a whole, to advise on the primary network and environmental area system, to give special attention to the problems (including redevelopment) arising in the central area, and to consider the balance between private and public transport'. A Report was made to the Council in January 1964 and in December 1965 there appeared in the bookshops *Bath: A Planning and Transport Study* by Colin Buchanan and Partners, although at a price of £4 it was hardly likely to reach a mass market.

The report is detailed, based on a great deal of evidence (published separately), and requires a certain amount of self-discipline if it is to be read right through. Like Abercrombie, Buchanan considers that even with the M4 there will be a substantial amount of through and visiting traffic but he asks for much bigger roads than Abercrombie's and, instead of sending the traffic thundering through the northern fringe of Georgian Bath, he sends it thundering down twin tunnels under the middle. The big roads, their intersection systems, and the tunnel aroused such a fury of opposition that it got into the national press and on to local television.

The trouble with a controversy such as this is that people of equal intelligence, sensitivity, and integrity can find themselves on opposite sides, and can also find themselves in strange and embarrassing company. It is not really soluble and this is because, as with any planning for the future, it deals in uncertainties. What makes it even more difficult is that if the scheme turns out to be a mistake it will have been an extremely expensive one, yet while the argument goes on costs are rising. It would seem that the only way of getting off the horns of a dilemma is to grasp the nettle danger and hope it does not sting you to death: if the metaphor is mixed, so is the problem.

In 1966 Colin Buchanan and Partners were at it again, this time for the Ministry of Housing and Local Government and the Bath Corporation, and in 1968 they produced *Bath: a Study in Conservation*. This was because Bath, along with Chester, Chichester, and York, had been designated as towns of particular historic interest and architectural value and each was to be reported on to examine how conservation policies might be carried out. The towns of course thought that the best way to help them to carry out conservation was to give them some money but so far this has not materialised.

Buchanan 2 deals, as instructed, with the central area and highlights a number of interesting problems, particularly in relation to the structural preservation and new use of buildings. The centre has suffered from a residential exodus which started in the nineteenth century and has accelerated. The result is that about 40 per cent of the space above ground-floor level is empty, with consequent deterioration as well as loss of revenue. The problems of making these spaces attractively habitable are formidable, particularly if access by car is to be limited, and Buchanan looks hopefully to student accommodation (incidentally, the Corporation has done an interesting conversion to the top storey of one side of Bath Street for use as Education offices). Another problem is that the old buildings have developed all kinds of unpleasant accretions on their backs, covering gardens, obscuring light, and cutting down ventilation and this is extremely difficult to deal with unless sufficient space can be created by restructuring the interior of the buildings. Good interior reconstruction can sometimes be done behind the old façade, as in the Paragon, but often the windows are in unsuitable places, the structure is too weak, and the floor levels are wrong.

Two recent examples which have created controversy are in Kingsmead Square and New Bond Street. Kingsmead Square, what with reconstruction, bombing, and traffic, is a mess, but the southern side still stands, decrepit but above ground floor much as it was at the beginning of the eighteenth century. There has been a variety of proposals and counter-proposals, developers have advanced and withdrawn in an endless dance as the buildings get worse and worse. Do we restore, or rebuild-as-it-was, or go modern? Similarly New Bond Street must be rebuilt before it collapses. But how? And although the various points of view have passionate protagonists, how many people really care? And how much are people prepared to pay? And how many people who sign petitions have any deep knowledge of the problems? Is the number who care increasing, are there many who care but are silent, and to what extent should the susceptibilities of those who care be considered? Should we agree with Buchanan that outside the areas of architectural homogeneity we should move boldly into the use of modern materials and styles, or should renewal and extension everywhere preserve past techniques and styles? And whence comes the authority for the categorical 'should'? The great democratic danger of trying to moderate between opposing views is that the outcome will be timid and weak, incapable of arousing either admiration or disgust, impotent to engender either love or hate.

There is the further problem that the Bath stone is particularly susceptible to atmospheric attack and much which was white and firm is now black and crumbling. In 1955 the Historic Buildings Council made grants available of 50 per cent of the cost of cleaning and repairing façades up to a yearly total of £10,000 (later increased to £20,000); the Corporation were to provide another 25 per cent and the owner of the building the remaining 25 per cent, which could cost up to £1,500. A major result of this has been the cleaning of the Circus and of parts of Pulteney Street with results which are pleasing to all except those who like their antiques hoary.

Overall planning was strengthened under the Town and Country Planning Act of 1947* when Bath became its own

* There were subsequent Acts in 1962 and 1968.

Planning Authority and had the statutory obligation to prepare a Town Map and Development Plan, but, as with most authorities, the City did not have the resources to carry out all the projects and the professional developer came increasingly into the picture, the role of the Authority developing more and more as one of laying down guide lines and passing judgement on submitted schemes, which in some cases have kept popping up like jack-in-the-boxes. The largest of these, the complete demolition and rebuilding of the area east of Southgate Street by Ravenseft Properties, has, in 1972, just begun. On the riverside site at the lower end of Walcot Street, work is already advanced on a new multi-storey car park and block of buildings to include a hotel and Law Courts. A smaller example, important because of its location, is the so-called 'Harvey' block at the north end of High Street, a flat-faced building whose towering top storey is coloured black, apparently in the belief that this renders it invisible. It is a love-or-hate building of which Buchanan appears to approve.

If decisions are to be taken which affect the lives of citizens then it seems reasonable, as the Skeffington report advocated in 1969, that the citizens should have the opportunity to obtain full knowledge of the facts and to express their opinion. In recent years, in addition to the usual Press services and publication of Council minutes, there have been public enquiries, public meetings, and an increased information service by the Council's planning department. Whether, as some would argue, this could be more adequate, is difficult to decide, as it is indeed for any information service. Any presentation involves selection and there is always room for argument about the appropriateness of the choice. Moreover agreement about content may not involve agreement about the way the content is expressed. There are other barriers to communication in the use of maps and models, for not everyone can translate these into real terms and, in any case, they are bound by their nature to be selective in what they show. Bath planning department display in their information centre in Abbey Green an admirable model of the city but on that scale we are looking at the city from an aeroplane and it is extremely difficult to interpret this in terms of a pedestrian's-eye-view. The use of different scales in time and place causes much disagreement and an answer which is right on one scale may at the same time be wrong on another. If granny's house is going to fall down in ten years' time it may, on a planning scale, seem eminently sensible to demolish it now and make way for redevelopment; on granny's scale this would be monstrous. To decide which is the better scale is an unenviable and probably impossible task.

With or without adequate knowledge, the expression of opinion requires the existence of pressure groups. These are often *ad hoc*, and in the history of Bath there has been no lack of people concerned enough to voice criticism and proffer advice. The most permanent and largest body (some 700 members at present) is the Bath Preservation Trust which developed from the Old Bath Preservation Society. It speaks with an influential, although not always unanimous, voice and has widened its terms of reference to include not only preservation but also the larger question of environmental quality. Its efforts have, amongst other things, led to the restoration and rehabilitation of one side of Beaufort Square, the restoration of No. 1 Royal Crescent and its furnishing and opening for visitors, and the recent acquisition for restoration of a shockingly dilapidated property in Abbey Green. It has also spoken for the tunnel scheme and then against it on the grounds that the original road plan has been changed.

Physical planning in Bath is not just of local concern. The City scene has an international reputation and when a bit is knocked down the tremors travel wide, evoking responses which range from the Americas to the Antipodes. This means that conservation has cash value in terms of attracting visitors although any attempt to assess the financial return on investment in refurbishing the buildings

41 Technical College: post-war building

42 Ballance Street flats

43 Bath University, Phase I

44 The City and the Admiralty buildings

and indeed in providing other tourist amenities is bound to
be tentative and open to considerable argument. Providing
that the economic climate is favourable and tourist habits do
not drastically change there would seem to be a good
economic case for the City investing heavily in the tourist
industry. Coupled with this is the possibility of development
as a conference centre which is at present hampered by a
lack of sufficient meeting places and accommodation, circumstances which affect, for example, the Bath Festival
which is, to say the least, a valuable means of keeping Bath
in the public eye and ear.

The Festival idea is not new, for it was in the economic
blizzard of 1930 that Bath put on a pioneer Festival of the
Contemporary Arts, in which Albert Sammons played
Delius, John Ireland gave a piano recital, and Constance
Lambert spoke Edith Sitwell's verse to Walton's *Façade*
through a megaphone from behind a curtain, while in the
Library and Art Gallery you could see Epstein's head of
'Nan' and original manuscripts by Drinkwater, Arnold
Bennett, and George Bernard Shaw. Again in 1936 there
was a Spring Festival of The Arts of Three Centuries, a
more local affair, although it did include a recital by Harriet
Cohen. It was in 1938, however, that the Mayor of Bath
and C. B. Cochran got together with a group which
included John Gielgud, Somerset Maugham, Diana Duff
Cooper, H. A. Vachell, and Oliver Messell to plan an
annual 'Salzburg the Second'. Amid merry quips from
Councillors about 'Mr Cochran's Young Ladies' the work
went forward, but early in 1939 when £4,000 had been
collected it was decided that the organisers could not get
together the artists they wanted and decided to postpone
until July 1940, by which time Bath was busy with other
things. When that business was over Bath saw in 1948 the
first post-war Festival in the country. Organised by Bath
Assembly Ltd in association with the Arts Council, directed
by Ian Hunter for Glyndebourne, and under the patronage
of the 17-year-old Princess Margaret, who attended in the

New Look, it had *Il Sergalio* from Glyndebourne and Evelyn Laye and Leon Quartermaine in *School for Scandal*; neither production got rave notices, but *Punch* liked the whole occasion. Each year the Festival reappeared until in 1955, when it snowed in May, it lost £12,000. In 1956 and 1957 (when petrol was rationed during the Suez crisis) it was not held, but in 1958 Harold Holt took over the organisation, still with Ian Hunter as Artistic Director, Yehudi Menuhin appeared in the Festival for the first time, and John Gielgud gave a Shakespeare recital. Next year Menuhin took over as Musical Director until he withdrew in 1968. Various changes in direction and organisation have taken place since.

This occasion, gathering together in Bath artists of world reputation and putting Bath for a week in the national news, is not without its critics. Artists have been known to complain of poor facilities, there is no large, modern concert hall (indeed, the Festival spreads to Bristol and Wells), and tickets are expensive. It is said to be too esoteric, lacking in popular appeal, to be in Bath but neither for nor of the city. Every year there are attempts to establish a strong Second Festival, or Fringe, although this has not yet achieved the strength and prestige of the Edinburgh Fringe. Bath, it is said, hardly gives the impression of being *en fête* – the decking of the central area with flowers for louts to knock down and others to enjoy are for the Britain in Bloom competition and coincidental, however pleasant and welcome. A pleasant touch, but a small one, is the provision of an open-air bar in the Abbey churchyard. On the whole, in spite of the assembly of outstanding professionals and the efforts of dedicated amateurs, Bath life seems curiously untouched by the Festival and perhaps this is due to some uncertainty about its meaning and purpose.

It could be argued either that Bath is too slumbrous to be excited by Festival noises or that the city has a strong current of activity which is hardly rippled by a one-week burst of artistic endeavour. There is certainly no lack of amateur societies and although the old Royal Literary and Scientific Society dissolved itself in 1959 its demise was largely due to the rise of so many organisations catering for specialist tastes. It would be invidious to pick out any of these by name and impossible here to deal with them all, but it is reasonable to say that what they all lack, apart from enough money, is an adequate home where their varied activities can be brought together and a society of Societies established. In spite of strenuous efforts on a number of occasions Bath has not yet achieved an Arts Centre.

To revert to the tourist theme, it is obvious that this must continue to play a part, hopefully an increasing part, in the economy of the city, but it is not the only source of economic strength. Throughout its history Bath has shown a capacity for change and development. Aquae Sulis was brand new, so was Saxon Bath. The city to which society flocked in the eighteenth century was one of furious building activity, where new towns were being added and the old was being torn down and renewed. In the nineteenth century Bath was pushing itself into a modern age. The Roman spa died, the medieval woollen industry died, the monastery disappeared, the Georgian gambling heyday passed, the healing waters were for a time discredited, and yet every time there was a looking forward, not back, and there were people with the nerve to risk a step into the unknown. Bath has always been, and still is, a city of change.

For example, in 1972 manufacturing provided 9,000 out of the 42,000 jobs in the city (in round numbers) and Bath exports are to be found throughout the world. Hampered by site conditions, Bath products have tended to be specialist, depending on skill, ingenuity, and often original invention. Stothert's produce big stuff (dockside cranes for example) but are also important for pumps and vibrating rollers whose designs they pioneered; Horstmann's continue their founder's inventiveness; Cross's founded in 1920 by another inventor, specialise in particular problems, such as providing rings for the Concorde engine; Hygate Gears specialises in products requiring a high standard of accuracy; Rotork, started by Jeremy Fry in the basement of Widcombe Manor in 1957 and now occupying an unusual-looking factory in Brassmill Lane, produces a highly specialised line of electric valve operators. Hiring out cranes to the world may seem a curious project to be sited at Bath, but once again this was a matter of personal initiative and imagination, and G. W. Sparrow and Sons on a bit of land between the Avon and the Lower Bristol Road have developed since the war into one of Europe's largest crane-hire specialists. The old-established cabinet-making industry took a leap into the space-age when in 1969 Arkana Ltd on the Lower Bristol Road entered into the business of manufacturing plastic and fibreglass furniture with a pioneer technique of rotational casting. A new development for Bath has been the establishment on the southern heights of a shoe factory by Clark's of Glastonbury.

There are other concerns who have a right to be named and would include such diverse activities as publishing, building, civil engineering, electronics, and providing computer data, but enough has been said to show that there is something more to Bath than dreams of past glory. In what proportion industry can contribute to the future economic base is difficult to predict, particularly in view of the geography of the place, but it would seem that, lacking local advantages of site, materials, and power, it must owe any development to continued ingenuity, skill, and initiative.

It is not therefore inappropriate that one of the major post-war developments in Bath has been the arrival of a University of Technology.* In 1960 the Bristol CAT (College of Advanced Technology) was designated to become a University. In 1964 it was still looking for a home when Bath Corporation offered it a 140-acre site on Claverton Down which had previously been developed as playing fields – a sacrifice which aroused a good deal of local opposition – and in 1965 220 students moved in. Since then the

---

* In 1971 the title was changed to the University of Bath.

horizontal slabs of the new University (Robert Matthew, Johnson-Marshall and Partners) set on landscaped terraces have added a new and generally unobtrusive architectural element to the city. Student numbers have increased to 2,500 (1972) and it is proposed to add a student village – an interesting conception which holds the danger of isolating the student community from the town. Meanwhile down in Avon Street the latest block of the Bath Technical College is going up.

When we consider that in addition to its architectural and archaeological attractions and its splendid setting Bath has a cluster of establishments of higher education (university, technical college, teaching hospital, college of education, college of home economics, and, in nearby Corsham, college of art), a concentration of professional consultants, a two-hour rail link to London, easy access to motorways, and a ring of scenic and historic attractions, it would seem axiomatic that a developing aspect of its economy will be to act as host to conferences – if only it can solve its traffic problems, and provide enough hotel rooms with baths, a concert hall, and adequate meeting rooms. It might also consider a problem which London is finding acute – how to provide for all the young people who want to see the place and cannot afford to put up in hotels. Not that Bath is without its own youth – any image of the place as one crowded with old people being towed around in Bath chairs needs correcting. Although the last census showed the City as having rather more than the national average of old people it still had nearly a third of its population under the age of 25. In fact, Bath faces a problem which is afflicting all our towns, that of catering adequately for the needs of the teenager and the needs of the old.

One source of income to the City not yet mentioned may seem curious for an inland place in a rural setting for it is the Admiralty, or, as it is now less resoundingly called, the Department of Defence (Navy). For strategic reasons it moved from London in 1939, took over the Empire Hotel and various other places, and built itself huts at Foxhill by Combe Down. It has become the biggest single employer in Bath and is now expanding and consolidating its position with proposed new building. What will happen to the Empire Hotel, which is something of a grey elephant, remains to be seen.

A more considerable question mark hangs over the future in Bath. Ever since the charter of Richard 1 the City has had increasingly greater responsibility for its own government, a principle emphasised in the national reconstruction of 1888 which left the County Boroughs as administrative islands in County seas. Subsequent years added more and more responsibility – for health, for education, for planning – and also produced critics who maintained that the town/country division was no longer real, nor the size of many local authorities sufficiently strong economically to allow any real measure of independence. Various tinkerings took place with boundaries but a wholesale re-shaping of the system did not become official policy until the publication in 1969 of the report of the Royal Commission on Local Government which had been set up in 1966 under the chairmanship of Lord Redcliffe-Maud.

If the report had passed into law Bath would have lost all its powers to the Council of Unitary Area 37, a region made out of west Wilts, north Somerset, south Gloucester, and Bristol. Naturally the city objected. For other reasons there was a change of government at Westminster and the Maud proposals were dropped, to be replaced by the Local Government Act of 1972. By this Bath becomes in 1974 a District in the new County of Avon and although it can apply for and will doubtless obtain the right to continue with a Mayor and all the panoply of power it will lose a great deal of its responsibilities of government to the Avon County Council whose home is as yet undetermined. Bath has been unusually quiet about this latest change, most opposition having come from north Somerset where the 'Save Our Somerset' campaign lobbied strongly to keep out of Avon.

In every end is a beginning. Bath now faces a radical change in her administrative situation, a new power structure which requires the widest understanding and participation if it is to be used effectively to implement and direct the economic and environmental changes which are already in motion and are yet to come. The history of Bath shows a City of remarkable resilience and one whose citizens since the Georgian hey-day have shown a deep affection and concern for their home and whenever the wheels of change have shown signs of jamming there has been no lack of people to give them a kick – the danger being that equally hearty kicks from different directions can be as ineffectual and more damaging than no kicks at all.

If past history is anything to go by Bath will enter the next phase still very much alive – and still kicking.

BRIEF BIBLIOGRAPHY

Most of the material for this book has come from the study of original sources either at first hand or in transcript and these are mainly in the local collection at the Bath reference library where there is an excellent index and a knowledge-able staff. This material is not therefore listed here.

Many of the relevant books are out of print or difficult to obtain, and the following list is intended to do no more than to indicate some of the more recent and more readily available works.

Ball, A. *Yesterday in Bath*, 1972. The nineteenth century recreated in photographs of the time, together with an illuminating text.

Boyce, B. *The Benevolent Man*, 1967. An American account of the life of Ralph Allen, carefully researched and documented.

Clear, C. R. *John Palmer*, 1955. Well documented account of the mail-coach pioneer and his monumental row with the Postmaster General in 1792.

Coard, P. *Vanishing Bath*, Parts I and II, 1971. Delicate drawings of buildings, large and small, and details of their architecture with historical notes by Ruth Coard.

Cunliffe, B. *Roman Bath*, 1969. A definitive account of the excavations, finds, and reconstruction of the baths, temple, and other features.

Cunliffe, B. *Roman Bath Discovered*, 1971.

Gadd, D. *Georgian Summer*, 1972. A very readable account of eighteenth-century Bath.

Ison, W. *The Georgian Buildings of Bath*, 1970. This is a Kingsmead reprint of the work first published in 1948. It is definitive, detailed, and splendidly illustrated.

Little, B. *Bath Portrait*, 2nd ed., 1968. Of particular interest for the architectural history, it is also a very useful introduction to the general history of the city.

Panter, H. *Edgar*, 1972. In this clearly written little book a great deal of information relating to Edgar and his coronation are brought together.

Pevsner, N. *North Somerset and Bristol*, 1958. This volume of the Penguin series, Buildings of Britain, is the best introduction for the visitor to the buildings in Bath. Authoritative, good reading, this is a book to walk round with.

Smith, R. A. L. *Bath*, 1944. An engaging history written with much affection for the place.

Smithson, P. *Bath*, 1971. An analysis of snatches of townscape, thought-provoking and idiosyncratic.

Walters, J. *The Splendour and the Scandal*, 1968. A readable account of the life of Beau Nash.

Wood, J. *An Essay towards the Description of Bath*, 1968. This is a Kingsmead reprint of Wood's Essay of 1765.

Wroughton, J. (ed.). *Bath in the Age of Reform*, 1972. A collection of essays by Sixth Formers at King Edward's School, which sets a high standard of readability and scholarship and fills a gap in our knowledge of Bath.

INDEX

214 *Index*